RECOMMENDATIONS

Dr. Morey's speaking and writing ministry is recommended by some of the best-known Christian leaders in this generation.

Dr. D. James Kennedy (Coral Ridge Ministries)

"Dr. Robert A. Morey is an excellent speaker and writer on the subject of cults and the occult. His books are excellent resource tools on these subjects. It is my pleasure to recommend him to churches everywhere throughout our land."

Dr. John Ankerberg (The Ankerberg TV Show)

"I have known Dr. Robert Morey for a number of years and welcome this opportunity to recommend him to you. Dr. Morey is a man with an excellent understanding of the historic Christian faith and a particular skill as a defender of the Faith. I heartily recommend him to you."

Dr. Stephen Olford

"I praise the Lord that He has given you such a strategic ministry in the field of apologetics and theology. The Lord bless you richly."

Dr. Herbert Ehrenstein (Editor of Eternity Magazine)

"It is a genuine privilege for me to recommend Dr. Robert A. Morey as a competent Biblical scholar in the field of apologetics, Bible teaching and evangelism. I have known Dr. Morey for over 30 years and it has been a delight to me to see his developing a fantastic grasp of Biblical truth, and his unique ability to translate that exalted truth of God's Word into down-to-earth, meaningful and methodical ways his audiences can make use of it."

A Bible Handbook on Slander and Gossip

Dr. Robert A. Morey

For other exciting books by Dr. Robert A. Morey, contact:

Christian Scholars Press

PO Box 240

Millerstown, PA 17062

www.faithdefenders.com

The Bible, Natural Law, and Natural Theology: Conflict or Compromise?
Is Eastern Orthodoxy Christian?
The Islamic Invasion
Winning the War Against Radical Islam
The Trinity: Evidence and Issues
Death and the Afterlife
How the Old and New Testaments Relate to Each Other
The Nature and Extent of God's Knowledge
Fearing God
Studies in the Atonement
Battle of the Gods
Satan's Devices
The Encyclopedia of Practical Christianity
The Truth About Mason
How to Keep Your Faith While in College
The New Atheism and the Erosion of Freedom
An Introduction to Defending the Faith
When is it Right to Fight?
How to Answer a Jehovah's Witness
How to Answer a Mormon
Reincarnation and Christianity
Horoscopes and the Christian
Worship is All of Life
How to Keep Your Kids Drug-Free

Special thanks to Jon
Powell and Jessica
and Omar Garcia for
their help in preparing
the manuscript.

To all who suffer
slander and gossip:
Keep your eyes fixed
on Jesus (not on your
critics) and run the
race set before you for
"great is your reward
in heaven."

Table of Contents

Preface

Dr. Morey's handbook presents and discusses the biblical material, a plethora of passages dealing with gossip and slander beginning with its history in the Bible: Satan's innuendo slandering the Lord God in the beginning in Eden, the slandering of Job by Satan and the patriarch's so-called "friends", the slandering of Moses and Aaron by Korah, the slandering of Nehemiah by Sanballat, finally the slandering of Jesus by false witnesses. Then the author discusses the primary texts of Scripture on gossip and slander: Deuteronomy 19:15-21, Psalm 15:1-3 and Psalm 25:8-10, Matthew 18:15-22, 1 Timothy 5:15-21, and finally the passages in Proverbs on gossip and slander.

Dr. Morey's handbook is full of practical and valuable counsel on recognizing and responding (or not responding) to slander: for instance, 21 signs of how to recognize a gossip monger. Last but not least, what makes this little book especially valuable, are all the contemporary illustrations of gossip and slander, along with the application of biblical principles to them. These illustrations are drawn from Dr. Bob's long ministry and vast experience as a pastor and as a counselor of pastors (pastor pastorum) and their parishioners.

Dr. George P. Hutchinson, Th.M., D.Phil.

Introduction

The internet has proven to be both a blessing and a curse. As a blessing, it has enabled Christians to evangelize people in countries where evangelization is not legal. I have had many wonderful opportunities of witnessing through the internet to Muslims in Saudi Arabia, Qatar, Indonesia, and Singapore.

After emailing each other for several months, one dear Muslim in Turkey accepted Jesus as the Son of God and renounced Islam as based on a false god (Allah), a false prophet (Muhammad), and a false book (Qur'an). There are many faithful Christian sites that debate unbelievers and defend the glorious Gospel of the unmerited grace of God.

The internet has also been a curse because it is the #1 purveyor of pornography. Millions of minds have been polluted with vile images that degrade men, women and even children. Dr. James Dobson stated on "Focus on the Family" that up to 40% of pastors have fallen into the snare of internet porn. It has become one of the major problems in Christian counseling today.

I received a desperate call from a pastor of a large church near Seattle, Washington. So many men in his church had become addicted to internet porn that he was in a panic with how to deal with it. Sexual issues were so embarrassing to him that he needed to bring someone outside of his church who would deal with the issue bluntly. He asked several fellow pastors if they knew anyone who could deal with this issue with biblical faithfulness. After my name was suggested several times, he called me. He set up a special men's fellowship weekend during which I dealt with the issue of internet porn. God delivered many of the men that weekend.

While internet porn is a great problem today and must be dealt with by a clarion call to repentance, there is another form of internet "porn" that is far more wicked and vile. Internet slander and gossip sites and bloggers have become a greater curse against pastors and ministries today than pornography.

As documented by Peter Hammond/Brian Abshire[1], G. Lloyd Rediger[2], and Dr. Greenfied[3], some professing Christians today do not just leave a church when they disagree with the leadership of that church. They set up internet sites and blogs where they malign, slander, and gossip against the leadership and the church with the sole intent to destroy them. They are not interested in reconciliation or truth. They have no fear of God or of man. They engage in making up every lie imaginable and, when exposed, they continue to repeat the same lies over and over again. They are without conscience and have demonic energy to keep up their attacks year after year. They are malicious in their very core of being and thus reveal that they are actually *unregenerate*. They are the *tares* among the wheat.

One pastor wrote us that he was blessed when he went to our website[4] and found biblical material on how to handle being slandered. He had fired a church secretary and, instead of leaving and finding something positive to do for Christ, she set up a blog where, for several years she has slandered him, his wife, and his church. With satanic energy, she spends every waking moment inventing new lies and spreading gossip against him.

It was our joy to comfort him by pointing out:

(1.) He was not alone in being slandered on the internet.

(2.) It is now a worldwide phenomenon that afflicts all public figures (politicians, police, doctors, media stars, clergy, etc.).

(3.) The devil was a slanderer from the beginning.

(4.) It is thus no surprise that those inspired by him do likewise.

(5.) The answer is to give your reputation and ministry to God and trust in His sovereign protection.

(6.) Church history judges a pastor by his works - not by his critics.

My dear friend Dr. Gleason Archer shared this illustration with me one day. In the middle of the night, some malicious people threw snowballs against a granite wall. They stuck to the wall. But, when the sun rose in the morning, which fell down? The granite wall or the snow balls? The snow balls fell to the ground with the coming of the light. In the same way, false accusations will eventually fall to the ground as they are exposed to the light of the day. Therefore do not panic when people malign and slander you. Their accusations will eventually fall to the ground as the lies of the devil.

If you are a pastor, elder, deacon or missionary reading this book, do not be surprised when people hate and slander your good name and even attack your family. The devil has always used gossip and slander to attack God's servants. Indeed, Jesus warned us that if all men speak well of us, this may mean you are false!

> Woe *to you* when all men speak well of you, for in the same way their fathers used to treat the false prophets. (Luke 6:26)

Matthew Henry's comments are especially powerful because of the vile slander and gossip that attacked him, his father, and their ministries.

> You now undergo *the world's ill will.* You must expect all the base treatment that a spiteful world can give you for Christ's sake, because you serve him and

his interests; you must expect that wicked men will *hate you,* because your doctrine and life convict and condemn them; and those that have church-power in their hands will *separate you,* will force you to separate yourselves, and then excommunicate you for so doing, and lay you under the most ignominious censures. They will pronounce anathemas against you, as scandalous and incorrigible offenders. They will do this with all possible gravity and solemnity, and pomp and pageantry of appeals to Heaven, to make the world believe, and almost you yourselves too, that it is ratified in heaven. Thus will they endeavor to make you odious to others and a terror to yourselves. This is supposed to be the proper notion of *aphorisosin hymas* — *they shall cast you out of their synagogues.*

"And they that have not this power will not fail to show their malice, to the utmost of their power; for *they will reproach you,* will charge you with the blackest crimes, which you are perfectly innocent of, will fasten upon you the blackest characters, which you do not deserve; they will *cast out your name as evil,* your name as Christians, as apostles; they will do all they can to render these names odious.'""

This is the application of the eighth beatitude, Mt. 5:10–12.

Such usage as this seems hard; but *blessed are you* when you are so used. It is so far from depriving you of your happiness that it will greatly add to it. It is an honor to you, as it is to a brave hero to be employed in the wars, in the service of his prince; and therefore *rejoice you in that day, and leap for joy,* v. 23. Do not only *bear it,* but *triumph* in it. For," (1.) "You are hereby *highly dignified* in the *kingdom of grace,* for you are treated as the prophets were before you, and therefore not only need not be ashamed of it, but may justly rejoice in it, for it will be an evidence for you that you *walk in the same spirit,* and *in the same steps,* are engaged in the same cause, and employed in the same service, with them.'"" (2.) "You will for this be abundantly *recompensed* in the *kingdom of glory;* not only your services for Christ, but your sufferings will come into the account: *Your reward is great in heaven.* Venture upon your sufferings, in a full belief that the glory of heaven will abundantly countervail all these hardships; so that, though you may be losers for Christ, you shall not be losers by him in the end.'"

Here is a *woe* to them *whom all men speak well of,* that is, who make it their great and only care to gain the praise and applause of men, who value themselves upon that more than upon the favor of God and his acceptance (v. 26): "*Woe unto you;* that is, it would be a bad sign that you were not faithful to your trust, and to the souls of men, if you preached so as that nobody would be disgusted; for your business is to tell people of their faults, and, if you do that as you ought, you will get that *ill will* which never *speaks well.* The false prophets indeed, that flattered your fathers in their wicked ways, that *prophesied smooth things* to them, were caressed and spoken well of; and, if you be in like manner cried up, you will be justly suspected to deal deceitfully as they did.'" We should desire to have the approbation of those that are wise and good, and not be indifferent to what people say of

xiv

us; but, as we should despise the reproaches, so we should also despise the praises, of the fools in Israel.[5]

Chapter One

Twenty One Signs of a Gossip Monger

Internet slander and gossip are forms of pornography in that they pollute and defile the minds of internet "Peeping Toms" who love to read the latest gossip against pastors and churches. There are twenty one signs of an internet gossip monger.

1. **They never go in *private* to the pastors they slander in *public*.** They excuse their disobedience to Matt. 18 by various rationalizations. What is a "rationalization"? A lie dressed up as an excuse and served up as the truth. But, the fact remains that slanderers go *public* with their accusation without ever meeting in *private* with the pastors they slander. Sad to say, some pastors have fallen into the sin of gossip mongering. One "fellowship" of pastors met in secret and then publicly condemned a pastor of "abuse" without ever meeting with him! They did not even bother to send the pastor their public condemnation. When the pastor heard about their public condemnation, he asked for a copy of the accusations and the identity of his accusers. They refused to let him know either! When he appealed to Acts 25:16, they ignored God's Word. Like the Pharisees of old, they were ignorant of the Word and power of God. They were later put to shame for clearly violating dozens of Scriptures.

2. **They do not give the pastors the benefit of the doubt.** The pastors they attack are not "innocent

until proven guilty." Instead, they are guilty until they "prove" they are innocent. Gossip mongers lay the burden of proof on the accused, not on themselves. They hurl an accusation at a pastor and immediately hurl another one. They do not bother to prove any of their accusations with biblically valid evidence. One pastor was accused of being in the Mafia because he had a dear Italian friend. What is surprising is that several pastors wrote to him demanding that he prove that he was not in the Mafia!

3. **As soon as one of their lies is refuted, they invent a new one.** They either delete the refuted accusations from their website and deny they ever gave them in the first place or continue to repeat them knowing that internet "Peeping Toms" never check out the facts.

4. **They never apologize on their website or blogs when caught in lies.** A missionary was accused on the internet of stealing mission money. Even after accountants demonstrated beyond all doubt that he had not stolen one penny, the slanderers never apologized or asked for forgiveness.

5. **Their accusations are so vague that they are incapable of proof or disproof**. While preaching in Australia, one pastor asked me to help him deal with a woman in his church who was slandering him. She claimed that he "undressed her with his eyes" while he was preaching in the pulpit. She "felt" that he lusted after her in his heart. The pastor could not disprove her slander anymore than she could prove it. This is why "pastoral abuse" is a favorite accusation of slanderers. It is so vague that it cannot be disproven or proved. What one church calls "church discipline" another church calls "abuse." Korah used this satanic device against Moses. If the "abuse" is not moral or doctrinal but relates to such

2

issues as the hiring and firing of employees, it is not a valid accusation.

6. **They often have never met the pastor they are slandering and have never attended his church.** They do not have any first-hand information concerning him, his family or church. Their slanders are based solely on hearsay, rumors, and gossip. The gossipy fellowship of pastors mentioned before did not know the pastor they publicly condemn.

7. **They are guilty of the sin of "taking up an offense" of others (Psa. 15:3).** They will often admit that the pastor never did anything to them personally. He never stole their money or slept with their wife. They are angry at him because of what someone claims the pastor said or did to him. They go public with the slander they picked up from others.

8. **They never contact the leadership of the churches the pastor served to see what they think about their pastor.** The fellowship of pastors who slandered a pastor as "abusive" never bothered to ask all the churches he had pastored over a period of thirty five years. If they had done so, they would have found that they all supported the pastor as a faithful and loving pastor. No wonder the Book of Proverbs calls such people "fools."

9. **They depend on malicious slander from embittered ex-members who were put under church discipline for sin or who left in sympathy with those put under discipline.** To accept bitter accusations from those under discipline is like going to the money changers and the Pharisees for the "real truth" about Jesus! The witnesses brought forward by Korah against Moses and the witnesses produced by Sanballet against Nehemiah were

3

clearly malicious and thus invalid. People who are malicious and angry are *never* reliable witnesses. This is why Moses condemned malicious witnesses in Deut. 19.

10. **They do not have restoration and healing as the goal of their slanders**. Gal. 6:1 is quite clear that the only valid motive for attempting to deal with fellow Christians whom you "feel" have sinned against you or someone else, is to *restore* them in love to fellowship. Disgruntled ex-members who engage in slander and gossip against their former church and pastor have forgotten, "Vengeance is mine, says the LORD." Like the wolves described in John 10, their only motive is to hurt, kill, and destroy.

11. **Their blog or website is filled with "bitterness and wrath and anger and clamor and slander" (Eph. 4:31).** They mock and ridicule the pastor, his wife, his children, his church, and, in one case, even his dog! Their website or blog does not manifest the "wisdom from above" but the devilish "wisdom from below" (James 3:15-18). One test to judge whether a website or blog is godly is whether it increases faith, hope, and love in those who read it. If it produces anger and hate, it is of the devil. Does this blog or web site "refresh the hearts of the saints" or embitter them? (Phile. 1:7)

12. **They attack the motives, heart, and attitudes of the pastor.** When they cannot attack the doctrine or morals of a pastor, they attack him *personally*. Over the years we have comforted many pastors and missionaries who have been slandered for supposedly being mean, unloving, unkind, abusive, lustful, proud, conceited, greedy, etc. Such accusations clearly violate 1 Cor. 4:3f.

13. **They base their slander on accusations that have no first hand eye witnesses to support them or**

4

rely solely on single witnesses, malicious witnesses, and false witnesses. When their violation of Deut. 19:15f is pointed out to them, they don't care. They are naïve and gullible in the extreme.

14. **Their accusations cannot be disproved because you cannot prove a negative.** One pastor was slandered as being in the Mafia and being a Mason. The slanderers demanded that he "prove" that he was not in the Mafia or in the Masons! When it was pointed out to them that the burden of proof was on them, not the pastor, they did not respond.

15. **Internet gossip bloggers think that slander is their "ministry" and gossip their "spiritual gift." They think they are doing God a favor by slandering pastors.** But gossip and slander are always condemned in Scripture and never recommended as something Christians should do. They are "works of the flesh" and not "fruit of the Spirit."

16. **Bloggers and slanderers are often psychosexual stalkers.** Their sexual desires and fantasies about the pastor were not fulfilled and, in retaliation, they stalk him for years. Although the woman in Australia (who slandered her pastor for "undressing her with his eyes") left the church, she used the internet to accuse him of "immorality." Her accusations actually revealed her sexual fantasies about him, not his about her. One male slanderer has spent every waking moment for fifteen years slandering a Christian leader. Such an obsession is clearly "unnatural."

17. **Psychologists and psychiatrists have documented that those who engage in internet gossip and slander blogs often destroy their**

5

marriages. When the pastor they slander takes the high road and ignores the slanderers and bloggers, this infuriates them because they are psychologically desperate for his attention. When he ignores them, they become depressed, angry, and filled with hate. When they hear that the pastor is joy-filled and going on in his ministry, they become so angry that they take it out on their family. One psychosexual stalker, who had an unnatural desire for the attention of his pastor, was so enraged by the fact that the pastor ignored his slanders on the internet that he abused his wife and step-daughter until they left him. In another case, the wife repeatedly called the police to accuse her husband of assault and battery and even attempted murder! Hatred must have an outlet and, if it cannot kill the pastor, it assaults family members.

18. **Bloggers and slanderers think about the pastor they are attacking every moment of the day.** They constantly think up new ways to attack him and his family. They are psychologically obsessed with him. They cruise the internet looking for new accusations they can spread. They form web-groups that have the pastor's destruction as their only goal in life.

19. **When their malicious accusations fail to destroy the pastor, they invent bizarre accusations that even their most ardent supporters realize have gone too far.** When a pastor continued in joyful ministry and his church continued to support him, despite his being accused of "all manner of evil," the slanderers tipped their hand by claiming that the pastor was unqualified for ministry because his little dog would jump up on visitor's laps to be petted! Supposedly, the dog was "unruly" and this disqualified the pastor from ministry! Given enough time, slanderers always reveal their malicious nature.

20. **Those who do nothing positive for Christ will always criticize those who do.** Slanderers and bloggers do not evangelize the lost or comfort the saints. They do not spend their time, energy, and money sharing the gospel with sinners but slandering the saints. Their work is evil and produces only evil. They forget that church history always judges a pastor by his works - not by his critics.

21. **The "sins" they attribute to pastors are not sins according to the Bible.** One slanderer accused a pastor's wife and son of "stealing ministry money." He argued that it was theft for the church to pay their car insurance! In this particular case, they happened to pay their own car insurance. But there is no Scripture that condemns giving health and auto insurance coverage to the pastor's wife and children. Another gossip monger claimed that it was "sin" for the pastor to store the offering in his safe over Sunday night until it could be deposited Monday morning. Where is this condemned in the Bible? Gossip mongers never seek biblical warrant for their accusations. It never occurs to them that they have to prove from the Bible that what they claim is a sin *is* a sin. One pastor was told that the slanderers would be willing to meet with him under one condition: he was not allowed to bring his Bible with him or refer to it at any point!

James was right when he said that those who slander the saints have tongues set on fire with the fire of hell (James 3:5-12). As we shall see, the Bible describes slander and gossip as sins worthy of excommunication and exclusion from the fellowship of the church. They are placed at the top of the list of wickedness along with murder and heresy. Why? Slanderers murder the reputation of the saints and rape the Bride of Christ!

7

Chapter Two

The Biblical History of Slander

Satan is called "the Accuser" in Rev. 12:10 because making malicious and slanderous accusations against God and His servants has always been the way that he opposes God.

The Fall of Man

In Genesis 3, Satan slandered God by accusing Him of evil motives and lying to man. Eve first fell into sin by listening to these slanders and receiving them as true. Eve turned against God because of the devil's slander and gossip against God. *Thus the root causes of the Fall of man into sin and guilt was slander and gossip!* This is why Satan is called, "The Slanderer" in Rev. 12:10. Since we have dealt in depth with the Fall in another book, we refer the reader to that discussion. [6]

The Book of Job

The Book of Job is the first canonical revelation of God and is also the first revelation of the person and work of Satan. How did Satan oppose God? He slandered the heart and motives of Job!

Job 1:9-11 Then Satan answered YHWH, "Does Job fear God for nothing? Haven't you made a hedge of protection around him, his family, and all that he possesses, on every side? You have blessed the work of his hands, and his possessions have increased in the land. But if put forth your hand now and touch all he possesses; he will surely curse you to your face."

Commentaries:

Satan responded by attacking Job's motives: **Does Job fear God for nothing?** "For nothing" (ḥinnām) is rendered "without any reason" in 2:3. Because Satan could not deny God's assessment of Job's godliness, he questioned *why* Job was pious. The accuser suggested that Job was serving God not out of love but only because of what he got from God in return. If Job's rewards were removed, out would go his reverence.

Satan suggested that if God removed His protecting **hedge around** Job and removed **everything he** owned, then Job would **curse** God. Job, Satan claimed, would no longer insert his coins of worship if nothing came out of the machine. Job, in other words, was worshiping for selfish reasons. This accusation also attacked the integrity of God, for it suggested that the only way He can get people to worship Him is to promise them wealth. [7]

See how slyly he censured him as a hypocrite, not asserting that he was so, but only asking,

10

"Is he not so?" This is the common way of slanderers, whisperers, backbiters, to suggest that by way of query, which yet they have no reason to think, is true. Note, It is not strange if those that are approved and accepted of God be unjustly censured by the devil and his instruments; if they are otherwise unexceptionable, it is easy to charge them with hypocrisy, as Satan charged Job, and they have no way to clear themselves, but patiently to wait for the judgment of God. [8]

Satan responded to Yahweh's question with one of his own. "Does Job fear God for nought?" Thus the arch slanderer accused the patriarch of ulterior motives. Satan could not deny that Job was in fact a godly man. But *why* was he godly? The allegation is that Job is being paid by God through a life of ease and prosperity to be pious. Here is the fundamental issue in the book. Do men serve God for who he is? Or for what he does for them? Will a person worship God without personal gain? Is worship essentially selfish? (1:9). [9]

Satan insinuates that Job's motive is purely selfish. He

serves God, not for love of God, or for love of goodness, but for what he gets by it. Satan is too shrewd to endeavor, as Job's friends do later, to pick holes in Job's conduct. No; that is exemplary. But the true character of acts is determined by the motive. What is Job's motive? Does he not serve God to gain his protection and blessing? Similarly, in modern times, ungodly men argue that religious and devout persons are religious and devout with a view to their own interest, because they expect to gain by it, either in this world, or in the next, or in both. This is a form of calumny which it is impossible to escape. And bad men, who are conscious to themselves of never acting except from a selfish motive, may well imagine the same of others. It is rarely that such an insinuation can be disproved. In the present instance God vindicates his servant, and covers the adversary with shame, as the other adversaries and calumniators of righteousness will be covered at the last day. [10]

Job 2:4 And Satan answered YHWH and said, "Skin for skin! Yes, all that a man has he will give for his life."

Commentaries:

In Satan's second test he again indicted God's words and impugned Job's motives and character (cf. 1:6-8). The Hebrew for **without any reason is** ḥinnam, the same word **Satan** had used in 1:9. Though **Satan** accused **Job** of having an ulterior motive in his worship, **God** threw this back at the accuser, saying that Satan had *no* reason to incite God against the patriarch. In this third scene, back in heaven, **Satan** implied that Job was still worshiping God because he had not yet given up his life. **Skin for skin! A man will give all he has**—posse-ssions and children—**for his own life.**" Skin for skin" was a proverbial saying, possibly about bartering or trading animal skins. Satan insinuated that Job had willingly traded the skins (lives) of his own children because in return God had given him his own skin (life). This again implied that Job was selfish. [11]

Satan, that sworn enemy to God and all good men, is here pushing forward his malicious prosecution of Job, whom he hated because God loved him, and did all he could to separate between him and his God, to sow discord and make mischief between them, urging God to afflict him and then urging him to blaspheme God. One would have thought that he had enough of his former attempt upon Job, in which he was so shamefully baffled and disappointed; but malice is restless: the devil and his instruments are so. Those that calumniate good people, and accuse them falsely, will have their saying, though the evidence to the contrary be ever so plain and full and they have been cast in the issue which they themselves have put it upon. Satan will have Job's cause called over again. The malicious, unreasonable, importunity of that great persecutor of the saints is represented (Rev. 12:10) by his accusing them before our God day and night, still repeating and urging that against them which has been many a time answered: so did Satan here accuse Job day after day. [12]

Satan's second question accuses God of placing a thorny hedge around Job, his family and his possessions thereby protecting him from pain and hardship. Then Satan pointed out that God had blessed all the work of Job's hand thereby increasing (lit., causing to burst out) his substance in the land (1:10).

The stage was now set for Satan's challenge. "Put forth your hand now, and touch all that he has, and he will curse you to your face!" Yahweh then put all of Job's possessions into the power of the evil one. Satan was restricted, however, with regard to touching the person of Job. Armed with this warrant, Satan "went out from the presence of Yahweh" (1:11). [13]

Exegesis and Application of the Passage

While Satan's slander against Job in heaven was unsuccessful, he was successful in slandering Job on earth. What happened to Job is a paradigm of what slanderers do today.

- Job's "friends" first got together in secret and gossiped against Job to each other behind his back.

15

25

- Since they could not find any false teaching or immoral behavior in his life to criticize, they focused on attacking his character and motives.

- They did not go alone to him in private but came as a "lynch mob" howling for his blood.

- Their purpose was to force Job to admit that the evil that came upon him and his family was divine punishment for sin. They did not seek to comfort him. They did not even bring him a crust of bread or ointment for his sores.

- When Job defended himself, they condemned him for doing so. If he did not defend himself, he would be admitting that he was guilty as charged. But if he did defend himself, this "proved" he was guilty as charged. This put Job in a "no win" situation.

- This trick is used when a slanderer accuses a pastor of pride. If he denies that he is proud, he is guilty of pride. If he does not object, he is guilty. He is damned either way!

- Throughout the book, they assumed Job was guilty. They did not give Job the benefit of the doubt.

- They had already made up their mind that there was nothing Job could say that would change their mind. Job was wasting his breath defending himself before the lynch mob that confronted him.

- Job was outnumbered and outgunned by his accusers. Slanderers and gossip mongers always feel safe in a mob. This is why Korah, Sanballet, etc. gathered people to their cause *before* they confronted the leader.

- God's revelation vindicated Job by condemning his "friends" and humbling them before Job.

- Job forgave them, prayed for them, and offered sacrifices on their behalf.

Satan was the real Source of all the accusations against Job. He hated Job because he hated Job's God.

Korah's Slander Campaign Against Moses and Aaron

Num. 16:1-3 Now Korah, (the son of Izhar, the son of Kohath, the son of Levi), and Dathan and Abiram, (of the sons of Eliab), and On, (the son of Peleth, of the sons of Reuben), gathered a group of men and confronted Moses, with certain of the children of Israel, two hundred and fifty princes of the assembly, famous in the congregation, men of renown. They all gathered themselves together against Moses and against Aaron, and said to them, *"You have exercised* too much authority by yourselves. Everyone in the congregation *is just as* holy as you, every one of them. And YHWH *is* among them just as much as you claim He is with you. Why then do you exalt yourselves "above" the congregation of YHWH?"

Commentaries:

> **The presumptuous Korah** (Num. 16:1–50)

> 1. *Korah's accusation* (Num. 16:1–3, 13–14): Korah and a group of rebellious Israelites accuse Moses of the following:

>> a. he is a dictator;

>> b. he has brought the Israelites into the wilderness to kill them;

>> c. he has been unable to bring them into the Promised Land.

> 2. *Moses' answer* (Num. 16:4–12, 15–30)

>> a. To the rebels (Num. 16:4–12, 15–22): Moses tells the rebels to show up the next day at the Tabernacle entrance with their incense burners. Then the Lord will show them who is holy and set apart for him.

>> b. To the rest (Num. 16:23–30): Moses warns the people to stay clear of the

18

troublemakers   if   they want to continue living.

3. *The   Lord's   anger* (Num. 16:31–50)

a. At the ringleaders (Num. 16:31–40):   The   very ground where they are standing opens up and swallows them alive! Fire blazes from the Lord and burns   up   Korah's followers who are offering incense.

b.   At the rest (Num. 16:41–50):

(1)   The rebellion (Num. 16:41–42):   The next   morning people   confront Moses and Aaron, saying, "You two have   killed   the LORD's people!"

(2)   The   response (Num.   16:43–46): The Lord sends a plague   on   the people to destroy them.

(3)   The rescue (Num. 16:47–50):   Aaron burns incense and makes   atonement for the people in

19

order to stop the plague. Before it stops, 14,700 Israelites die. [14]

At some point during the Kadesh encampment Moses and Aaron faced a serious challenge to their leadership. The dissidents were Korah, a Levite, and Dathan and Abiram of the tribe of Reuben. These rebels were joined by 250 princes.

The three leaders and their followers came to Moses and Aaron as a group. They accused the brothers of taking more authority than was rightfully theirs. The slogan of the dissidents was this: "The whole congregation is holy." Every Israelite was thus holy and the Lord was with them just as much as he was with Moses and Aaron. The brothers therefore had no right to set themselves over the assembly (15:3).

In the face of this attack, Moses fell facedown in an attitude of prayer. How long he remained in that position is not stated. After the prayer experience Moses announced a test which would prove who had the right to approach God as worship leaders. In the morning

Korah and his company must do what had heretofore been the exclusive prerogative of Aaron's family: they must burn incense before the Lord. Whoever could burn incense before the Lord without being destroyed by the fire of God's holiness would prove that he had been divinely chosen for priestly ministry. Moses concluded this challenge by using the very words of the rebels: You Levites have gone too far! Moses hoped thereby to (1) reveal who were the real instigators of the rebellion; and (2) drive a wedge between the conspirators (16:4–7).

Moses then met with the Levites separately. He was attempting to sever their association with Korah and his Reubenite allies. He reminded the Levites of the noble ministry to which God had called them. God had separated them from the rest of the congregation, and had brought them near to himself to do the work at the Lord's Tabernacle and to minister before the people. He warned them that by seeking the priesthood they were attacking the Lord, not Aaron (16:8–11).

Moses next summoned the Reubenites to a confrontation,

but they refused to meet with him. They repudiated Moses' leadership by accusing him of (1) leading them out of a land flowing with milk and honey into a barren desert; (2) lording it over them; (3) failing to deliver on his promise to lead them to a land of abundance; and (4) attempting to blind others to the true circumstances so that he could retain his leadership (16:12–14). [15]

Korah was a Levite who was not content to assist in the tabernacle; he wanted to serve as a priest as well (v. 10). Of course, this attitude was a direct rebellion against the Word of God as given by Moses, since it was God who made the tabernacle appointments. Not content to rebel alone, Korah gathered 250 princes of Israel, well-known men (most of them probably Levites), as well as three men from the tribe of Reuben, Jacob's firstborn son. In name, number, unity, and attitude, those rebels seemed to have a strong case against Aaron and Moses. It appears that Korah and his followers defied Aaron, while Dathan, Abiram, and On (being descendants of Reuben, the firstborn) questioned the authority of Moses. However, they were united in their plot.

22

Rebels rarely give the real reason for their attacks; in v. 3 the men argued that all of the nation was "a kingdom of priests" (Ex. 19:6), and therefore Moses and Aaron had no right to take the places of leadership. Of course, this rebellion was based on self-seeking and envy. These men wanted to "lift themselves up" before the congregation. Certainly the whole nation was holy to God, but He had placed some people in positions of leadership as He willed. The same is true of the church today: all saints are beloved of God, but some have been given spiritual gifts and spiritual offices for the work of the ministry (Eph. 4:15–16; 1 Cor. 12:14–18). We are encouraged to "desire spiritual gifts" (1 Cor. 14:1) but not to covet another person's spiritual office. If a believer wants a place of spiritual leadership, let him prove himself worthy of it by his character and conduct (1 Tim. 3:1ff). The church must heed Paul's warning in Acts 20:28–31.

Moses and Aaron did not defend themselves; they let God do the defending. Moses instructed Korah and his followers to bring censers (pots for burning incense) to the tabernacle where God would

23

demonstrate who was right in the dispute. He called for Dathan and Abiram to come, but they defied Moses' authority and refused to obey. In v. 25, Moses went to them, but his visit meant condemnation, not blessing. Note how the men blamed Moses for their failure to enter the Promised Land (vv. 13–14), when it was their own unbelief that brought this defeat. To rebel against Moses meant rejecting the Word of God, for he was God's prophet; and to rebel against Aaron meant rejecting the work of God on the altar, salvation by the blood. [16]

The rebellion against Moses and Aaron. The rebels were led by men of high standing. Korah was a Levite of the Kohathite clan, which cared for the ark and the vessels of the sanctuary. The Reubenite with him also belonged to a noble family. They were joined by 250 princes of the community, who had been called to the council and were well known among the people. Their complaint was against the hierarchy; they were claiming equal status with Moses and Aaron. This, therefore, was a challenge to the order imposed by God at Sinai (chs. 3–4). They were seeking the priesthood too

24

(10). Moses' words, *you and all you followers have banded together* (11), contain a play on words. 'Banded together' is a Hebrew word connected with the name Levi. When Moses summoned them, the heart of their resistance spilt out. They contradicted the covenant promises of God in a double way (13–14): they described Egypt as the land flowing with milk and honey (a description which God had given to Canaan), and they complained that Moses and Aaron had failed to bring them into the promised inheritance.

16:16–35 Judgment on the rebels. The Lord did not acknowledge Korah's party. He addressed Moses and Aaron only. We are told later in the record that the elders were standing with Moses (25). The assembly was commanded to separate from the rebels' tents 'or you will be swept away because of their sins' (26). When the judgment came, however, it became evident that mere separation was not enough. They fled in terror (34), resembling Lot's escape from the ruin of Sodom and Gomorrah (Gn. 19:17). [17]

At some unidentified place and time in the desert wanderings, **Korah,** a Levite, and **Dathan and Abiram,** of the tribe of Reuben, began to lead an uprising **against Moses.** They recruited **250** of the top **leaders** of Israel as collaborators. The tribal affiliations of the two main conspirators (Levi and Reuben) show that this was a rebellion against both the religious and political leadership of Moses. Thus **Aaron** the high priest also became an object of their attack.

Their discontent centered on the allegation that Moses and Aaron were unjustified in setting themselves over all the people since, by virtue of Israel's being **the LORD's** covenant **community,** all of them were equally **holy** and capable of being leaders. What they had neglected to point out was that the Lord Himself had appointed Moses and Aaron to their offices.
18

when Moses heard it, he fell upon his face—This attitude of prostration indicated not only his humble and earnest desire that God would interpose to free him from the false and odious imputation, but also his strong sense of the daring sin involved in this proceeding. Whatever feelings may be entertained respecting Aaron, who had formerly headed a sedition himself [Nu 12:1], it is impossible not to sympathize with Moses in this difficult emergency. But he was a devout man, and the prudential course he adopted was probably the dictate of that heavenly wisdom with which, in answer to his prayers, he was endowed. [19]

Evidently there was first a conspiracy that brooded in secret. The original agitators, Korah, Dathan and Abiram, succeeded in drawing to their party representatives from the whole congregation, princes of the particular tribes. Thus they arose against Moses and Aaron. Their cry to these two leaders: **enough for you**, may not be translated by the cool language: let what has been hitherto suffice you. It is a *quo usque* of indignation. To it is attached pretension in quite a radical form. When Moses falls on his face it is because he is in the greatest extremity and needs a divine decision, and looks for it. And on this decision reposes his exceeding bold and surprising answer. Not he will decide, but Jehovah. Let them all present themselves before Jehovah, the next morning even, as would-be priests, with censers, in order to stand before Jehovah along with Aaron in opposition and in rivalry, then Jehovah Himself will decide. According to the law, even the sons of the priests were forbidden to offer strange fire to Jehovah, much more were mere Levites and non-Levites forbidden to sacrifice, let alone to perform the holiest act of offering which was done in the very Sanctuary of the Tabernacle. Hence Moses could not have instituted such measures as he did here, had he not regarded the law as completely broken and suspended. His expedient reminds us of the words of Jesus to Judas: "that thou doest do quickly." With the congregation seduced as it was, Moses could not act with its support; the law could only be restored again by a mighty judgment of God. Still the rebels were not to be left in doubt about the great irony that lay in the admission of this candidating, hence the addition, in which he repeats the word of the Levites as a rebuking echo: **it is enough with you**, upon which follows a reproof. **Hear, ye sons of Levi**, *etc.*, ver. 8. Now he brings home to the Levites that they themselves had received from Jehovah—not from him—a prerogative above that of the other tribes of Israel, by which he lays bare the contradiction in their revolutionary watch-word. He charges them with untruthfulness; it was not the universal priesthood that they wanted, but they were emulous of the high-priesthood of Aaron (vers. 9, 10). Ye rebel, he says, against Jehovah Himself, not, as ye suppose, against Aaron, for he as a man signifies nothing in this business, that ye should murmur against *him* (ver. 11). In other words: your would-be murmuring against Aaron is a rebellion against Jehovah. [20]

Korah desired to take control of the Israelite camp with the aid of his associates Dathan, Abiram, and On, usurping the roles of both Moses and Aaron. [21]

As was so often the case, Moses' response before this band of rebels was that of a true servant prophet. He fell upon his face before the people as he prayed for wisdom from above, surrendering his will to that of his God. His response to Korah came after an unspecified period of time, but when he arose his words were poignant. Moses would leave it up to God to vindicate the relative holiness of the various parties through an experimental test involving a priestly ritual, a function to which the insurgents aspired. Only one whom God himself deemed qualified to serve in the priestly role would be granted access to serve in the capacity of an incense bearer. Any attempt by one who is not holy to perform such cultic ritual resulted in grave consequen-ces. According to Lev 10:1–2, even the priests (Nadab and Abihu, sons of Aaron) who offered incense improper-ly were subject to judgment by death. [22]

Exegesis and Application of the Passage

Step One: Korah was chosen and trusted by Moses to take some of the burden of administration off his shoulders (Exod. 18:19f and Num. 16:8f). Pastors are usually betrayed by the very people they hire to help them run the ministry. This has been called the "Judas syndrome." If Moses, Paul, and even Jesus were betrayed by people whom they trusted to help them in ministry, why should we assume that it will not happen to us?

Step Two: At some point Korah became angry at Moses and Aaron. From his accusations against Moses and Aaron, he felt that they were guilty of pastoral abuse, pride, and conceit. He thus sinned by judging their motives (1 Cor. 4:5). He did not charge them with false teaching or immorality. He "felt" that they "thought" they were "above" him and the people and they were more holy than anyone else. He, Korah, was just as holy as they were and he had just as

30

much right to offer sacrifices as they. He hated them and his anger motivated him to begin a smear campaign against them.

Step Three: Did he go to Moses and Aaron in private *before* saying anything to others? No. This was another sin.

Step Four: Korah slandered Moses and Aaron to Dathan, Abiram, and On. Their first sin was listening to gossip and slander from a single witness who was malicious and then they committed the sin of taking up Korah's offense against Moses and Aaron. Did they go in private to Moses and Aaron? No. That was another sin.

Step Five: This "fellowship" of leaders now sinned against Moses and Aaron by gossiping and slandering them to as many people as possible. Too often ministerial associations fall into the sins of gossip and slander and spend more time on such evils than prayer!

Step Six: They deceived "two hundred and fifty princes of the assembly, famous in the congregation, men of renown" by "smooth and flattering speech" (Rom. 16:18). Did any of them go to Moses and Aaron in private to check out the accusations? No. They violated Pro. 25:8-10 and fell into sin by "taking up" the offense of Korah (Psa. 15:3). Notice that no one accused Moses and Aaron of false teaching or immorality. Their accusations focused on "abuse of power," i.e. pastoral abuse. It is always easy to attack the policies and procedures of a local church, such as its church discipline or issues relating to the church staff, because they are relative to the situation.

Step Seven: They "gathered themselves together against Moses and Aaron," i.e. they held secret meetings during which they tried and convicted Moses and Aaron of sin without Moses and Aaron being aware of the accusations or given the opportunity of answering them.

Step Eight: They then went public with their accusations against Moses and Aaron before letting them know what

31

those accusations were or who was making them. They violated Acts 25:16.

Step Nine: Moses and Aaron did not know of these men or their secret meetings until *after* they had gone public with their slander. Korah falsely assumed that they did not need to prove their accusations. From what they said to Moses and Aaron, they assumed they were guilty.

Step Ten: Moses tried to meet with the rebels in private but they refused.

Step Eleven: Moses and Aaron were sickened and grieved at the wicked and sinful accusations against them. It was obvious that their accusers were not interested in reconciliation since they had already tried and convicted them in secret. Notice that Moses and Aaron did not fall into the trap of trying to answer their groundless accusations. It would have been a waste of time.

Step Twelve: Moses and Aaron went in prayer before the Lord and asked God to vindicate them from these false accusations. It hurt them deeply that the people they had chosen to help them in the ministry now betrayed them and attacked their motives and character. One key to see the difference between the righteous and the wicked in slander situations is to observe who manifests the fruit of the Spirit and who manifests "the works of the flesh" (Gal. 5:19-23). One supporter of a ministry under attack interviewed its staff and pastor and then visited the people who were slandering them. He found the slanderers full of hate and bitterness and the ministry staff and pastor loving and gracious. He continued his support of the ministry. "By their fruits you will know them."

Step Thirteen: God vindicated Moses and Aaron by terrible judgments against the leaders of the smear campaign. Over the years we have seen terrible judgments fall on those who slander the work of God. God's wheel may move slowly but they eventually grind the wicked to dust.

Step Fourteen: Even after God vindicated Moses and Aaron, they did not rejoice when their accusers fell under the wrath of God. They prayed for their enemies and asked God to have mercy on them (Num. 16:46f).

Sanballat's Smear Campaign Against Nehemiah

Neh. 2:10, 19 And when Sanballat the Horonite and Tobiah the Ammonite official heard *about it*, it was very displeasing to them that someone had come to seek the welfare of the sons of Israel...But when Sanballat the Horonite, and Tobiah the Ammonite official, and Geshem the Arab heard *it*, they mocked us and despised us and said,

> "What is this thing you are doing?
>
> Are you rebelling against the king?"

Neh. 4:1-15 But it came to pass, when Sanballat heard that we were rebuilding the wall, he became angry and developed great indignation, and mocked the Jews. And he spoke before his brethren and the army of Samaria, and said,

> "What are these feeble Jews doing?
>
> Will they fortify themselves behind walls?
>
> Will they begin to sacrifice in a temple again?
>
> Will they finish their work in a day?
>
> Will they revive the stones out of the heaps of the rubbish which
>
> are burned?"

Now Tobiah the Ammonite *who was with* him, said,

> "If a fox go up on what they build,
>
> he shall even break down their stone wall."

Nehemiah's prayer:

> "Hear, O our God, what they are saying; for we are despised: and return their reproach upon their own head, and give them for a prey in the land of captivity: And cover not their iniquity, and let not their sin be blotted out from before thee: for they have provoked *thee* to anger before the builders."

Thus we decided to rebuild the wall; and the wall was going to be joined together in the middle: for the people had a mind to work.

But it came to pass, *that* when Sanballat, and Tobiah, and the Arabians, and the Ammonites, and the Ashdodites, heard that the walls of Jerusalem were going to be repaired, *and* that the breaches in the wall were going to be closed, they became very angry. So, they conspired all of them together to come *and* fight against Jerusalem, and to hinder the work. Nevertheless we made our prayer to our God, and set a watch against them day and night, because of them.

And Judah said,

> "The strength of the bearers of burdens is decayed, and *there is* much rubbish; so that we are not able to build the wall. And our adversaries said,

> "They shall not know, neither see, till we come in the midst among them, and slay them, and cause the work to cease."

And it came to pass, that when the Jews which dwelt by them came, they said unto us ten times,

> "From all places whence ye shall
> return unto us *they will be upon
> you*."

Therefore set I in the lower places behind the wall, *and* on the higher places, I even set the people after their families with their swords, their spears, and their bows. And I looked, and rose up, and said unto the nobles, and to the rulers, and to the rest of the people,

> "Be not afraid of them: remember
> the Lord, *which is* great and
> terrible, and fight for your
> brethren, your sons, and your
> daughters, your wives, and your
> houses."

And it came to pass, when our enemies heard that it was known unto us, and God had brought their counsel to nought, that we returned all of us to the wall, every one unto his work.

Neh. 6:1-15 Now it came to pass, when Sanballat, and Tobiah, and Geshem the Arabian, and the rest of our enemies, heard that I had rebuilt the wall, and *that* there was no breach left therein; though at that time I had not set up the doors upon the gates; that Sanballat and Geshem sent unto me, saying,

> "Come, let us meet together in
> *some one of* the villages in the
> plain of Ono."

But they thought to do me mischief. And I sent messengers unto them, saying,

> "I *am* doing a great work, so that I
> cannot come down: why should
> the work cease, whilst I leave it,
> and come down to you?"

35

Yet they sent unto me four times after this sort; and I answered them after the same manner. Then sent Sanballat his servant unto me in like manner the fifth time with an open letter in his hand; Wherein *was* written,

> "It is reported among the heathen, and Geshem saith *it, that* thou and the Jews think to rebel: for which cause thou buildest the wall, that thou mayest be their king, according to these words. And thou hast also appointed prophets to preach of thee at Jerusalem, saying, *There is* a king in Judah: and now shall it be reported to the king according to these words. Come now therefore, and let us take counsel together."

Then I sent unto him, saying,

> "There are no such things done as thou sayest, but thou feignest them out of thine own heart."

For they all made us afraid, saying,

> "Their hands shall be weakened from the work, that it be not done."

Now therefore, O God, strengthen my hands.

Then I perceived that surely God had not sent him, but he uttered *his* prophecy against me because Tobiah and Sanballat had hired him. He was hired for this reason, that I might become frightened and act accordingly and sin, so that they might have an evil report in order that they could reproach me. Nehemiah's prayer:

36

"Remember, O my God, Tobiah and Sanballat according to these works of theirs, and also Noadiah the prophe-tess and the rest of the prophets who were *trying* to frighten me."

Commentaries:

When Sanballat the Horonite (perhaps meaning he was from Beth-Horon about 15 miles northeast of Jerusalem) and his associate **Tobiah,** from Ammon, **heard** that Nehemiah had arrived on the scene to help Israel, they were **very** displeased. Immediately they began to plan how to stop Nehemiah from achieving his goal. Perhaps they were hoping to gain control of Judah. In fact in the Elephantine papyri written in 407 B.C., 37 years after this event, Sanballat was called "governor of Samaria." But Nehemiah's motivation remained undaun-ted. He knew that God had brought him to this moment in Israel's history and he was about to tackle a project that others, for almost 100 years before him, had been unable to complete. [23]

When the official caravan arrived, it was bound to attract attention, particularly among those who hated the Jews and wanted to keep them from fortifying their city. Three special enemies are named: Sanballat, from Beth Horan, about twelve miles from Jerusalem; Tobiah, an Ammonite; and Geshem, an Arabian (Neh. 2:19), also called "Gashmu" (6:6). Sanballat was Nehemiah's chief enemy, and the fact that he had some kind of official position in Samaria only made him that much more dangerous (4:1–3).

Being an Ammonite, Tobiah was an avowed enemy of the Jews (Deut. 23:3–4). He was related by marriage to some of Nehemiah's co-laborers and had many friends among the Jews (Neh. 6:17–19). In fact, he was "near of kin" ("allied") to Eliashib the priest (13:4–7). If Sanballat was in charge of the army, then Tobiah was director of the intelligence division of their operation. It was he who gathered "inside information" from his Jewish friends and passed it along to Sanballat and Geshem. Nehemiah would soon discover that his biggest problem was not the enemy on the outside but the compromisers on the inside, a problem the church still faces today. [24]

As noted earlier (2:10) **Sanballat** was displeased when he **heard** that Nehemiah had returned to Jerusalem to help the Jews. Sanballat, however, did not know of God's interest in His people. Sanballat's displeasure turned to intense anger (4:1; cf. v. 7). So with **his associates,** including Tobiah (2:19; 4:3; also cf. v. 7; 6:1, 12, 14) and Geshem (2:19), and **in the presence of** Samaritan soldiers, Sanballat **ridiculed the Jews.** He accused them of rebelling against King Artaxerxes (2:19) and by a series of questions he suggested they were incapable of completing the project (4:2). Calling them **feeble** he asked if they would **offer sacrifices.** That is, could they possibly complete the walls so that they could then give sacrifices of thanksgiving? The question about finishing **in a day** suggests that the Jews did not know what they were undertaking. And how, Sanballat asked, could they use **burned,** weakened bricks from the **heaps of** debris? **Tobiah the Ammonite** (cf. 2:19), standing nearby, also tried to discourage the Jews. Ridiculing them, he said they were so inept in their work that **a fox,** weighing only a few pounds, **would break** it down by merely climbing **up on it.** [25]

4:1–5 Ridicule. Sanballat and Tobiah here amplify their mockery of 2:19 in an attempt both to demoralize the builders (5) and to reassure their own supporters (2). Nehemiah's response (4–5) was to commit the problem to God in prayer, which is commendable, for he thereby recognized that the insults were directed as much against God as against himself and that vindication should come from his LORD rather than his own efforts. [26]

Ridicule (Neh. 4:1–6)

British critic and author Thomas Carlyle called ridicule "the language of the devil." Some people who can stand bravely when they are shot at will collapse when they are laughed at. Shakespeare called ridicule "paper bullets of the brain," but those bullets have slain many a warrior.

It is not unusual for the enemy to insult the servants of God. Goliath ridiculed David when the shepherd boy met the giant with only a sling in his hand (1 Sam. 17:41–47). Jesus was mocked by the soldiers during His trial (Luke 22:63–65) and by the rabble while He was hanging on the cross (23:35–37); and some of the heroes of the faith had to endure mocking (Heb. 11:36). *When the enemy laughs at what God's people are doing, it is usually a sign that God is going to bless His people in a wonderful way.* When the enemy rages on earth, God laughs in heaven (Ps. 2:4).

Sanballat and his friends had begun to ridicule the Jews even before the work on the wall had begun. "They laughed us to scorn," wrote Nehemiah, "and despised us" (Neh. 2:19). What special relationship Sanballat had with the army of Samaria is not explained to us. Perhaps he had the army assembled as a show of strength to frighten the Jews. By making his initial speech before the army, Sanballat intensified the power of his ridicule as he made some important people laugh at the Jews.

First, Sanballat ridiculed *the workers* by calling them "feeble Jews" (4:2). The word *feeble* means "withered, miserable." The people were like cut flowers that were fading away. They had no human resources that people could see, but the enemy could not see their great spiritual resources. The people of the world don't understand that God delights in using feeble instruments to get His work accomplished (1 Cor. 1:18–31). The world glories in its wealth and power, but God's people glory in their poverty and weakness. When we are weak, then we are strong (2 Cor. 12:1–10).

Then Sanballat ridiculed *the work itself* by asking three taunting questions. "Will they fortify themselves?" must have evoked gales of laughter from the Samaritan army. How could a remnant of feeble Jews hope to build a wall strong enough to protect the city from the army? "Will they sacrifice?" implies, "It will take more than prayer and worship to rebuild the city!" This question was blasphemy against Jehovah God, for Sanballat was denying that God would help His people. "Will they finish in a day?" suggests that the Jews didn't know how difficult the task was and would soon call it quits.

In his final question, Sanballat ridiculed *the materials* they were using. The stones were taken out of the rubbish heaps and probably were so old and damaged that they would never last when set into the wall. While it is true that limestone is softened by fire, it is also true that the walls were "broken down," while the gates were "consumed with fire" (Neh. 2:13). In spite of what Sanballat said, there was still plenty of good material for the builders to use.

Tobiah the Ammonite was one of the visiting dignita-ries at the Samaritan army inspection; and when it was his turn to make a speech, he ridiculed *the finished product (4:3).* You wouldn't need an army to knock down the wall; a solitary fox could do it! Of course, much that Sanballat and Tobiah said was true *from a human point of view;* for the Jewish remnant was weak and poor, and the work was too great for them. But they had great faith in a great God, and that's what made the difference.

How did Nehemiah respond to this ridicule? *He prayed and asked God to fight the enemy for him.* This is the third time you find Nehemiah praying (1:4–11; 2:4), and it will not be the last time. Nehemiah didn't allow himself to get detoured from his work by taking time to reply to their words. The Lord had heard the sneering taunts of Sanballat and Tobiah, and He would deal with them in His own way and His own time.[27]

God's people always have enemies. In this case, they were Sanballat, a government official in Samaria; Tobiah, the Ammonite; and Geshem, an Arabian, who is also called Gashmu (6:1, 6). These three wicked men were outside the nation of Israel; in fact, the Ammonites were definite enemies of the Jews (Deut. 23:3–4). Their first weapon was ridicule; they mocked the "feeble Jews" openly before the leaders of Samaria. Satan is a mocker (Luke 22:63; 23:35–37). Ridicule is a device used by ignorant people who are filled with jealousy. They mocked the people ("feeble Jews"), the plan ("will they finish in a day?"), and the materials ("stones and rubbish"). How did Nehemiah answer them? He prayed to his God! His concern was only for the glory of God and the testimony of the nation, so do not read personal revenge into his prayer (see Ps. 139:19–24). Note that the people still worked as they prayed, for prayer is no substitute for work. Satan would have loved to see Nehemiah leave the wall and get involved in a dispute with Sanballat, but

Nehemiah did not fall into Satan's trap. Never allow ridicule to stop your ministry; "take it to the Lord in prayer" and keep on working.[28]

Intimidating plots (Neh. 4:7–9)

A common enemy and a common cause brought four different groups together to stop the work on the walls of Jerusalem. The city was now completely surrounded by enemies! To the north were Sanballat and the Sama-ritans; to the east, Tobiah and the Ammonites; to the south, Geshem and the Arabs; and to the west, the Ashdodites. Ashdod was perhaps the most important city in Philistia at that time, and the Philistines did not want to see a strong community in Jerusalem.

God's people sometimes have difficulty working together, but the people of the world have no problem uniting in opposition to the work of the Lord (Ps. 2:1–2; Acts 4:23–30; Luke 23:12). As the enemy saw the work progressing, they became angry and decided to plan a secret attack against Jerusalem. Satan hates the Jews and has used one nation after another to try to destroy them (see Ps. 85 and Rev. 12). God chose the Jews to be His vehicle for giving the world the knowledge of the true God, the Scriptures, and the Savior (Rom. 9:1–5). "Salvation is of the Jews" (John 4:22), and Satan wanted to prevent the Savior from coming into the world. If he could destroy the nation, he would frustrate God's plan.

Nehemiah suspected that his enemies would launch an attack, so he posted a guard and encouraged the people to pray. The workers held both tools and weapons (Neh. 4:17) and were prepared to fight when the signal was given. "Watch and pray" combines faith and works and is a good example for us to follow in our work and our warfare (see Mark 13:33; 14:38; Eph. 6:18; Col. 4:2–4).

The Christian's battle is not against flesh and blood, but against Satan and his demonic forces that use flesh and blood to oppose the Lord's work. If we hope to win the war and finish the work, we must use the spiritual equipment God has provided (Eph. 6:10–18; 2 Cor. 10:1–6). If we focus on the *visible* enemy alone and forget the *invisible* enemy, we are sure to start trusting our own resources; and this will lead to defeat.[29]

Nehemiah didn't pay much attention to these complainers but went right on with the work. That's the best thing to do. If you take time away from your work to listen to everybody who wants your attention, you will never get anything done. Nehemiah got his encourage-ment from prayer and the promises of God, and the occasional complaints of some of the people didn't upset him.[30]

When we face a situation that creates fear in our hearts, we must remind ourselves of the greatness of God. If we walk by sight and view God through the problems, we will fail, as did the Jews at Kadesh-Barnea (Num. 13:26–33). But if we look at the problem through the greatness of God, we will have confidence and succeed. That was the approach David took when he faced Goliath (1 Sam. 17:45–47).

When the enemy learned that Jerusalem was armed and ready, they backed off (Neh. 4:15). God had frustrated their plot. "The Lord brings the counsel of the nations to nothing; He makes the plans of the peoples of no effect. The counsel of the Lord stands forever, the plans of His heart to all generations" (Ps. 33:10–11, NKJV). It is good to remind ourselves that the will of God comes from the heart of God and that we need not be afraid.[31]

After praying, Nehemiah and the Jews continued with the work. Some Christians pray and then wait for things to happen, but not Nehemiah! As in all his efforts, he blended the divine perspective with the human. He faced Sanballat's opposition with *both* prayer and hard work. Once he committed the problem to the Lord, he trusted God to help them achieve their goal. And while praying and trusting, they **rebuilt the wall** to **half its height.** At this juncture their task was half completed. Sanballat and Tobiah's efforts at demoralizing the Jews failed.[32]

The Jewish workers' rapid progress naturally incre-ased the threat to their enemies, who became **very angry** (cf. v. 1). So they decided to take more overt and corporate action. Joining **Sanballat** and the Samaritans from the north, **Tobiah** and **the Ammonites** from the east, Geshem (cf. 2:19) and **the Arabs** from the south, were **men** from **Ashdod,** a Philistine city, from the west. **They all plotted together to** attack **Jerusalem,** apparently from all sides.

The corporate strategy of Judah's enemies was met by a corporate response. Again the people **prayed** for help, and then added action to their prayers by posting **a guard** round the clock **to meet this threat.**[33]

Exegesis and Application of the Passage

The "passage of full mention" on Satan's device of slander is the Book of Nehemiah. It illustrates the scope and dimensions of how Satan slanders men of God and thus hinders their ministry. Pastors would be wise to study and then preach on Satan's devices or schemes by which he seeks to destroy churches and their pastors. [34]

First, Nehemiah understood that all the hatred and animosity directed at him had to do with the fact that he was the man of God called to do the work of God. There was nothing personal in these attacks. Anyone who does the work of God will be attacked by the devil and his crowd.

Second, Satan always finds some fool who will do his bidding. Be it Korah, Sanballat, Judas or Demas, there are always people who think that destroying a pastor and his ministry is their "ministry."

Third, the same pattern of slander used by Korah is now repeated by Sanballat. This "pattern" is the device or scheme that Satan uses over and over again. It worked in the Garden with Eve, and it has been a favorite tool of the devil ever since. Seminaries and Bible Colleges should teach young men entering the ministry to be on their guard for this device.

Fourth, Sanballat became angry at Nehemiah and used slander and gossip to oppose him. He accused him of crimes such as treason and revolution to get the government to persecute him. When legal and political means did not prevail to stop Nehemiah, he did a mass mailing of letters to spread slander about Nehemiah far and wide. Today, slanderers use the internet instead of letters to deceive naïve and gullible people into joining their crusade to stop pastors. It is clear that they do nothing positive with their time and talents. They spend all their time attacking the man of God and his ministry.

Fifth, Nehemiah ignored their slanders and gossip and did not waste time arguing with them. He had more important things to do with his time and energy. Trying to answer slander and internet gossip is like walking outside and picking up a feather off the ground and declaring, "I am going to find the bird where this feather came from." It would be a waste of time. Instead, do what God called you to do and let God and others defend you.

Sixth, the more you do what God has called you to do, the more they will slander you. This reveals that the real issue is what you are doing, not who is doing it.

Seventh, don't be upset by the ridicule and mocking of the devil and his crowd. They will mock you for such things as your physical appearance (2 Kings 2:23). I have seen pastors slandered for being too good looking or too ugly, too fat or too thin. So, don't take such cheap shots seriously.

Eight, some of the people became depressed because of the ridicule, slander, accusations, and intimidations against their leader. They may like their pastor and, know in their hearts that he is a good man and not the monster the slanderers make him out to be, but they abandon him in his hour of need because they grew tired of the controversy. Pastors must do what they can to encourage the sheep not to run away because of the growling of the wolves. Those who abandon their pastor never regain the joy they once knew until they go back to him and ask him to forgive them for betraying him. I have seen this truth over and over again in many churches.

Ninth, Sanballat wasted his life in the shadow of Nehemiah's accomplishments. He never got a life of his own. He followed Nehemiah around and criticized what he did or did not do. This is why they ridiculed Nehemiah's work. Those who never accomplish anything positive for God, always resent those who do.

Tenth, Sanballat, like Korah, assumed there was strength in numbers. The more fools he recruited for his crusade against Nehemiah, the more vindication he felt. One pastor foolishly thought that if he could deceive several other foolish pastors to join him in slandering another pastor he had a grudge against, the more righteous was his cause. In the end, he was exposed as a gossip monger and a liar. If he would have used the energy and time he spent in gossip and slander on evangelizing sinners, he would have converted most of his community!

The Slander Campaign against Jesus

Matthew 11:19 The Son of Man came eating and drinking, and they say, 'Behold, a gluttonous man and a drunkard, a friend of tax-gatherers and sinners!'

Mark 3:21-22 And when His own people heard *of this*, they went out to take custody of Him; for they were saying, "He has lost His senses," and the scribes who came down from Jerusalem were saying, "He is possessed by Beelzebul," and "He casts out the demons by the ruler of the demons."

Commentaries:

That commonly those persons who do not profit by the means of grace, are perverse, and reflect upon the ministers by whom they enjoy those means; and because they do not get good themselves, they do all the hurt they can to others, by raising and propagating prejudices against the word, and the faithful preachers of it. Those who will not comply with God, and walk after him, confront him, and walk contrary to him. So *this generation* did; because they were resolved not to believe Christ and John, and to own them, as they ought to have done, for the best of men, they set themselves to abuse them, and to represent them as the worst. (1.) As for John the Baptist, they say, *He has a devil.* They imputed his strictness and reservedness to melancholy, and some kind or degree of a possession of Satan. "Why should we heed him? he is a poor hypochondriacal man, full of fancies, and under the power of a crazed imagination." (2.) As for Jesus Christ, they imputed his free and obliging conversation to the more vicious habit of luxury and flesh-pleasing: *Behold a gluttonous man and a wine-bibber.* No reflection could be more foul and invidious; it is the charge against the rebellious son (Deu. 21:20), *He is a glutton and a drunkard;* yet none could be more false and unjust; for Christ *pleased not himself* (Rom. 15:3), nor did ever any man live such a life of self-denial, mortification, and contempt of the world, as

Christ lived: he that was *undefiled, and separate from sinners,* is here represented as in league with them, and polluted by them. Note, The most unspotted innocency, and the most unparalleled excellency, will not always be a fence *against the reproach of tongues:* nay, a man's best gifts and best actions, which are both well intended and well calculated for edification, may be made the matter of his reproach. The best of our actions may become the worst of our accusations, as David's fasting, Ps. 69:10. It was true in some sense, that Christ was *a Friend to publicans and sinners,* the best Friend they ever had, for he *came into the world to save sinners,* great sinners, even the chief; so he said very feelingly, who had been himself not a *publican and sinner,* but a Pharisee and sinner; but this is, and will be to eternity, Christ's praise, and they forfeited the benefit of it who thus turned it to his reproach.[35]

Jesus, then, is saying, "That is the way you, Phari-sees and your followers, are behaving. You are being childish. You are frivolous and are acting irresponsibly, inconsistently. You are never satisfied. You used to be filled with enthusiasm about John; at least, you stood in awe of him and did not find fault with his austerity and call to repentance. But now you say, 'He is too harsh and unsociable; his message is too severe. Why, he must be possessed.' But you are also turning against me, the Son of man. You are pointing the finger at me and saying, 'Though he demands self-denial in others, he himself is a glutton and a drinker, a friend of tax-collectors and sinners. He is too sociable.' "

Jesus points out that in the end such thoroughly unfair and bitter criticism and intolerance will get nowhere. The victory is on the side of truth. [36]

Meanwhile a delegation of Law **teachers** (scribes) **came down from Jerusalem** to investigate Jesus. They repeatedly charged (a) that **He** was **possessed by Beelzebub** (demon-possessed; cf. v. 30), and (b) that **He** was **driving out demons** through a power alliance with Satan, **the prince** (ruler) **of demons** (cf. v. 23).

3:23-27. Jesus summoned His accusers and refuted their charges **in parables** (short proverbial sayings, not stories). He dealt with the second accusation first (vv. 23-26) by showing the absurdity of their underlying assumption that **Satan** acts against **himself.** He used two illustrations to make the self-evident point that **if a kingdom** or **a house** (household) **is divided against itself** in purpose and goals, it **cannot stand.** The same applies to Satan if it is assumed that **Satan opposes** himself **and** his realm **is divided.** This would mean that **his end has come,** that is, his power, not his personal existence. Clearly this is false, for Satan remains strong (cf. v. 27; 1 Peter 5:8). So the charge that Jesus' exorcisms were due to Satan's power was false.[37]

Even the family of Jesus thought that he must be *out of his mind.* Many of God's most faithful servants, from Paul down to John Sung, the great evangelist of south-east Asia, have faced this same charge. But the *teachers of the law* who must have come *down from Jerusalem* on a special commission of enquiry, went further in their spite. They said that Jesus was not mad, but demon-possessed.[38]

The charge leveled against Jesus by scribes and Pharisees

was wicked. It was the result of envy. Cf. Matt. 27:18. They felt that they were beginning to lose their following, and this they were unable to endure. How completely different had been the attitude of John the Baptist (John 3:26, 30). The thoroughly shameful character of the charge becomes apparent also from the fact that it regards Beelzebul not as an evil spirit exerting his sinister influence upon Jesus from the outside; no, Beelzebul is regarded as being inside the soul of Jesus. The latter is said to *have*—that is, to be possessed by—this unclean spirit (Mark 3:22, 30; cf. John 8:48). The charge, then, amounts to this, that Jesus, indwelt by and in league with Satan, is by the power derived from that evil spirit driving out demons.

Christ's reply follows in verses 23-30, which may be divided as follows: *a.* refutation of the charge (verses 23-26); *b.* explanation of Christ's demon expulsions and other miracles (verse 27); *c.* exhortation (verses 28-30).[39]

Exegesis and Application of the Passage

Jesus was slandered as being immoral, a drunk, a glutton, blasphemous, demon-possessed, a traitor who sought the violent overthrow of Rome, and rejecting Moses.

56

Many "witnesses" were brought forward at his trial who verified that all these accusations were true.

If the enemies of Messiah could manufacture such malicious slanders against Him, why should we be surprised if we are not also hated and maligned?

Matthew 10:24-25 A disciple is not above his teacher, nor a slave above his master. It is enough for the disciple that he become as his teacher, and the slave as his master. If they have called the head of the house Beelzebul, how much more the members of his household!

John 15:18-19 If the world hates you, you know that it has hated Me before *it hated* you. If you were of the world, the world would love its own; but because you are not of the world, but I chose you out of the world, therefore the world hates you.

Pastors and missionaries should realize that Jesus said to take up their cross daily because they would be crucified daily! Those who are on the frontlines of spiritual warfare against the kingdom of darkness will be slandered by the devil and his crowd. You know when you are bombing the enemy's headquarters by the amount of flack that comes up against you.

Slandering the Resurrection

Matthew 28:11-15 Now while they were on their way, behold, some of the guard came into the city and reported to the chief priests all that had happened. And when they had assembled with the elders and counseled together, they gave a large sum of money to the soldiers, and said, "You are to say, 'His disciples came by night and stole Him away while we were asleep.' And if this should come to the governor's ears, we will win him over and keep you out of trouble." And they took the money and did as they had been instructed; and this story was widely spread among the Jews, *and is* to this day.

Commentaries:

1. They *put money into their hands;* and what wicked-ness is it which men will not be brought to by the love of money? They *gave large money,* probably a great deal more than they gave to Judas, unto *the soldiers.* These chief priests loved their money as well as most people did, and were as loath to part with it; and yet, to carry on a malicious design against the gospel of Christ, they were very prodigal of it; they gave the soldiers, it is likely, as much as they asked, and they knew how to improve their advantages. Here was *large money* given for the advancing of that which they knew to be a lie, yet many grudge a little money for the advancement of that which they know to be the truth, though they have a promise of being reimbursed in the resurrection of the just. Let us never starve a good cause, when we see a bad one so liberally supported.

2. They *put a lie into their mouths* (v. 13); *Say ye, His disciples came by night, and stole him away while we slept;* a sorry shift is better than none, but this is a sorry one indeed. (1.) The sham was *ridiculous,* and carried

along with it its own confutation. If *they slept,* how could they know anything of the matter, or say who came? If *any one* of them was awake to *observe it,* no doubt, he would awake them all to *oppose it;* for that was the only thing they had in charge. It was altogether improbable that a company of poor, weak, cowardly, dispirited men should expose themselves for so inconsiderable an achievement as the rescue of the dead body. Why were not the houses where they lodged diligently searched, and other means used to discover the dead body; but this was so thin a lie as one might easily see through. But had it been ever so plausible,   (2.) It was a wicked thing for these priests and elders to hire those soldiers to tell a deliberate lie (if it had been in a matter of ever so small importance), against their consciences. Those know not what they do, who draw others to commit one willful sin; for that may debauch conscience, and be an inlet to many. But, (3.) Considering this as intended to overthrow the great doctrine of Christ's resurrection, this was a sin against the last remedy, and was, in effect, a blasphemy *against the Holy Ghost,* imputing *that* to the roguery of the disciples, which was done by *the power of the Holy Ghost.* It would take a *large sum of money* to persuade the soldiers to spread the cover-up story, as sleeping on guard duty was a capital offence. But Pilate's reputation was well known; if the story reached his ears, he could be *satisfied* with a further bribe. Justin mentions that such stories were still being circulated in the second century to discredit the fact of the empty tomb.[40]

Exegesis and Application of the Passage

How did Satan seek to overturn the glorious news of the bodily resurrection of Messiah? Did he produce the body of Jesus or other hard evidence? No. Instead of refuting the testimony of the eyewitnesses, Satan spread the slander and gossip that the women and the apostles were thieves and liars. The slanderers claimed they actually stole the body of Jesus out of the tomb and then covered their theft by the lie of the resurrection.

Matthew notes that this slander was still being circulated as he composed his Gospel account. How professing Christians can think that spreading slander and gossip is the work of God is beyond our comprehension. Anyone who engages in slander is delusional if he thinks he is doing God a favor.

Conclusion

In Heb. 11 we find that all the great men and women of biblical history were slandered and accused of many evil things. Subsequent church history records that all faithful ministers are accused of vile things. Athanasius and Calvin were accused of murder. Luther was slandered as mentally ill. Whitfield, Spurgeon, Edwards, etc. were all slandered and maligned by their enemies. Pastors must take to heart that accusations and slander are part of a faithful ministry (John 15:18-2; 2 Tim. 3:12).

Chapter Three

Primary texts

The Bible in *hundreds* of passages refers to slander and gossip as abominations before God. Certain passages directly deal with this wickedness and thus they are the primary passages in God's Word that explain the nature and wickedness of slander and gossip. It will profit us greatly to examine these primary texts.

Deut. 19:15-21 A single witness cannot accuse anyone of any iniquity or any sin that he has supposedly committed. But only on the sworn testimonies of two or three credible eye witnesses shall an accusation be allowed. If a malicious witness accuses someone of wrongdoing, then both the men who have the dispute shall stand before the Lord, before the priests, and the judges who will be in office in those days. The judges shall investigate thoroughly, and if the witness is a false witness and he accused his brother falsely, then you shall do to him what he wanted done to his brother. Thus you shall purge the evil one from among you. The rest of the people will hear of this and become afraid, and will never again do such an evil thing among you.

Commentaries:

> This principle was to act as a safeguard against a false witness who might bring an untruthful charge against a fellow Israelite because of a quarrel or out of some other impure motive. By requiring more than one witness—at least **two or three**—

greater accuracy and objectivity was effected. **If** on investigation the testimony was found to be **false** then the accuser (**a malicious witness,** 19:16, and **a liar,** v. 18) received the punishment appropriate for the alleged crime. When the fate of the false witness became known in Israel it would serve as a great deterrent against giving false testimony in Israel's courts. Violating the ninth commandment (Ex. 20:16) was another **evil** to be purged from the nation. [41]

A single witness shall not be admitted to the condem-nation of an accused person.[42]

Here is a statute for the preventing of frauds and perjuries; for the divine law takes care of men's rights and properties, and has made a hedge about them. Such a friend is it to human society and men's civil interest.[43]

To secure life and property against false accusations, Moses lays down the law in v. 15, that one witness only was not "to rise up against any one with reference to any crime or sin, with every sin that one commits.[44]

Nothing is more dangerous than to expose men's lives to the tongue of a single individual.

Lest, therefore, any one should be oppressed by any light conjectures, or insufficient accusations, or unjust prejudices, God here interferes, and does not allow any to be harshly dealt with, unless duly convicted.[45]

One witness should not be enough to bring in a person guilty of a crime; however clearly that witness might say he saw the hand and the crime, yet his testimony should be sufficient to inflict condemnation on the person accused...Better that ten criminals should escape, than one innocent man should be condemned. And, therefore, it is laid down, that unless there are two, or even three, witnesses, no accused person shall be brought in as guilty of the crime laid to his charge.[46]

Exegesis and Application of the Passage

Israel was a pure theocracy in that God dictated the laws governing every aspect of life. Marriage, religion, dress, diet, morals, etc. were all prescribed by divine decree. The Torah embraced all of life because YHWH was Lord over all of life. There was no secular or neutral realm where God was prohibited.

The Lordship of YHWH was applied to the issue of when an accusation was deemed valid or invalid. This insight is important because we live in antinomian culture where people believe they are a law unto themselves. They can accuse anyone of anything and everyone should believe them and condemn the person they are accusing.

The internet has become the largest source of pornography in the world today. Many people today become addicted to porn through the internet. Gossip and slander are nothing more than verbal pornography. Thus it is no surprise that sexual and verbal porn dominate the internet and have ruined thousands of lives.

Slander and gossip rest upon the gullibility of people to believe a lie because it tickles their ears (2 Tim. 4:3). The lie is dressed up as an accusation that is leveled against someone. This accusation should be based on some hard evidence to support it or it should be dismissed at once. But gullible people do not even need one witness to believe an accusation. They will believe an accusation even when it does not have a single witness to support it.

1. **No Witness Accusations:** *Anonymous* accusations from *unnamed sources* are **never** valid. Today, groundless accusations are published on the internet that do not have even one eye witness to support them. For example, a disgruntled ex-member of a church accused his pastor of adultery on the internet. When the ex-member was asked for the name and contact information of any woman who had an affair with the pastor, he admitted that no woman had *ever* accused the pastor of having an affair with him! Yet, some pastors believed the evil report and spread the rumor in their pastor's fellowship.

2. **Single Witness Accusations**: An individual cannot accuse anyone of any sin if all the "proof" he has is what he claimed he heard or saw. "He told me on the phone" is no proof whatsoever. The disgruntled ex-member not only accused his pastor of adultery but also of stealing money from the offering plate. When he was asked for two or three eye witnesses who saw the

66

pastor take money from the offering plate, he said that he alone had seen it. But the pastor never took the offering, counted it, recorded it, deposited it or did anything with it. The pastor said that the ex-member was lying. Those who believed the single witness and condemned the pastor sinned against the pastor by violating not only Deut. 19 but also 1 Tim. 5:19.

3. **Malicious Witness Accusations**: The witness must be *credible*, i.e. he should not stand to gain anything from his accusations. The music director wanted to become the pastor and slandered the pastor in order to run him out of the church. Any accusations that are part of a plan or strategy to take over a church or to destroy a ministry are suspect. The accuser should not be emotionally motivated by hate or a spirit of vengeance. People who are filled with hate will invent all manner of evil to accuse an innocent man.

   A disgruntled ex-member had been put under church discipline by the Board of his church. But, instead of attacking the Board, he focused his slanders against the senior pastor. The ex-member's blog was filled with "bitterness and wrath and anger and clamor and slander" (Eph. 4:31). The language and spirit of his internet accusations sowed disunity and discord among the brethren. When you are confronted with someone who has an axe to grind against someone, you should not believe what he tells you.

4. **False Witness Accusations**: Just as single witnesses are usually malicious witnesses, malicious witnesses are usually *false* witnesses. The enemies of the prophets, apostles and Jesus invented many serious and vile accusations against them. For example, the man who had accused a Christian leader of theft, adultery, etc. had a partner who worked with him in their "gossip ministry." In the presence of two officially

67

designated witnesses, he confessed that he and his partner had deliberately made up the lies and asked the pastor to forgive him. Yet, even with the sworn testimony of these eye witnesses, some pastors chose to continue to believe the lies! When the Board of the ministry being slandered offered to present to his pastor all the bank evidence proving that the Christian leader was not a thief, he said that he did not care how many witnesses and how much evidence the Board had and refused to meet with them!

5. The severity of the punishment placed on anonymous, single, malicious, and false accusations reveals that slander and gossip are major sins that merit church discipline. Since death was the punishment under the Old Covenant, excommunication (i.e. purging from the congregation) is the punishment under the New Covenant.

6. Moses points out that if church discipline is administered on malicious accusers, the rest of the congregation shall take notice and refrain from gossip and slander. This benefit is repeated by Paul in 1 Tim. 5:20.[47]

Psa. 15:1-3 YHWH, who shall abide in your tabernacle? Who shall dwell in your holy hill? He that walks in integrity; and works righteousness, and speaks the truth in his heart, and does not slander with his tongue, nor does evil to his neighbor, nor takes up a reproach against his neighbor.

Commentaries:

> v. 3. He *does no evil* at all *to his neighbor* willingly or designedly, nothing to offend or grieve his spirit, nothing to prejudice the health or ease of his body, nothing to injure him in

his estate or secular interests, in his family or relations; but walks by that golden rule of equity, To do as he would be done by. He is especially careful not to injure his neighbor in his good name, though many, who would not otherwise wrong their neighbors, make nothing of that. If any man, in this matter, bridles not his tongue, his religion is vain. He knows the worth of a good name, and therefore *he backbites not,* defames no man, speaks evil of no man, makes not others' faults the subject of his common talk, much less of his sport and ridicule, nor speaks of them with pleasure, nor at all but for edifice-tion. He makes the best of everybody, and the worst of nobody. He does not *take up a reproach,* that is, he neither raises it nor receives it; he gives no credit nor countenance to a calumny, but frowns upon a backbiting tongue, and so silences it, Prov. 25:23. If an ill-natured character of his neighbor be given him, or an ill-natured story be told him, he will disprove it if he can; if not, it shall die with him and go no further. His *charity will cover a multitude of sins.*[48]

This strophe describes negatively his conduct towards his neighbor: (1) He does not go

69

about with slander upon his tongue. רגל = literally, to go about as a spy or tale-bearer, or slanderer. This is a wicked walk, the negative of the perfect walk, ver. 2*a.;* (2) he does not do evil; (3) he does not take up a reproach against his neighbor. נשא, according to Hupfeld, has here the meaning of "bring forth," "speak out," = *proferre, efferre.* Delitzsch, Hengst., Hitzig, *et al.,* give it the meaning of bringing or loading disgrace upon any one, Calvin, *et al.,* to lift up as from the ground. To this latter interpretation Perowne inclines: "He hath not stooped, so to speak, to pick up dirt out of the dunghill that he may cast it at his neighbor.[49]

The fact that there are 10 descriptions of one who qualifies to abide with the Lord (sincere, righteous, honest, without slander, without doing wrong, without reproaching, distinguishes between good and evil, keeps his oath, does not take interest, does not accept bribes) suggests a comparison with the Ten Commandments (though the two lists do not correspond in every item). Obedience to God's revealed will is the requirement for full participation in the sanctuary...A righteous person does not **slander** maliciously. (3) Nor does he harm or (4) discredit **his neighbor.** A neighbor (or friend) is anyone with whom he comes in contact. A blameless individual's remarks do not harm or destroy any neigh-bor.[50]

Those who are fit for communion with God may be known by conformity to His law, which is illustrated in various important particulars... He neither slanders nor spreads slander.[51]

Here is the holiness without which no one sees God (Heb. 12:14), covering conduct, conversation and relationships (2–3), values, integrity and financial con-tentment (4–5).[52]

The next qualification for entering the Temple has to do with *slander*, spreading malicious gossip or speaking ill of others. *Tongue* represents the organ of speech, and it is not necessary to say literally in English (as does RSV) *slander with his tongue.* In some languages, however, the literal phrase may be quite effective. Slander is sometimes expressed idiomatically as "taking away people's names", "saying bad words about people" or "putting dirt on people's backs". Reproach (TEV "rumors") translate a word meaning *taunt, scorn or contempt.*[53]

He that **backbiteth not with his tongue**. Among the negative virtues the first place is given to the observance of the ninth commandment, probably because to err in this respect is so very common a fault (see Jer. 6:28; 9:4; Jas. 3:5–8). **Nor doeth evil to his neighbor**; rather, *to his friend*, or *his companion*—a different word from that used at the end of the verse, and implying greater intimacy. There is special wickedness in injuring one with whom we are intimate. **Nor taketh up a reproach against his neighbor.** The good man does not, even when it is true, spread an ill report concerning his neighbor. He prefers to keep silence, and let the report die out (see Exod. 33:1).[54]

The prophet, for distinguishing of the true members of the church from those who were only outwardly professors, asketh of the Lord how the one may be known from the other...A third fruit of unfeigned faith, is making conscience in all his dealings, that he harm not his neighbor, neither in his name, nor in his person, nor his goods: and making conscience not to receive readily a false report of his neighbor, when it is devised by another.[55]

Note that the blameless lifestyle is characterized as: sincere, honest, avoids malicious speech, does nothing to harm or discredit another, avoids vile people, honors and keeps company with those who fear God.[56]

Lastly, he would refuse to "take up a reproach against his neighbor." This appears to imply taking up for the sake of gossip anything that may be uttered by way of defaming another's character.[57]

Slanderers are restless bodies and go about, spying out other peoples' affairs and spreading injurious or false reports...**nor taketh up a reproach against his neighbor**. The word rendered *take up* is elsewhere translated *bear, spare, accept, stir up, suffer, respect, exalt, contain, raise, regard, bring, help,* and often *lift up*. A good man is not willingly even the repository of evil rumors against any of his kind...Gill explains it that this good man "does not himself raise any scandalous report on his neighbor, nor will he bear to hear one from another,

73

much less will he spread one"...Mudge...Nor throweth a disgrace upon his neighbor.[58]

Scandal, reproach, defamatory accusation...The idea then is, that he has not helped to load his neighbor with reproach.[59]

In the first place, he tells them that they must not be slanderers or detractors; seconddly, they must restrain themselves from doing anything mischievous and injurious to their neighbors; and thirdly, they must not aid in giving currency to calumnies and false reports...If a good name is a treasure, more precious than all the riches of the world, (Pro. 22:1), no greater injury can be inflicted upon men than to wound their reputation...Some take the phrase, to raise up a calumnious report, for to invent, because malicious persons raise up calumnies from nothing; and thus...good men should not allow themselves to indulge in detraction. But I think there is also here rebuked the vice of undue credulity, which, when any evil reports are spread against our neighbors, leads us either to eagerly to listen to them, or at least to receive them without sufficient reason; whereas we ought rather to use all means to suppress and trample them under foot. When anyone is the bearer of invented falsehoods, those who reject them leave them, as it were, to fall to the ground; while, on the contrary, those who propagate and publish them from one person to another are, by an expressive form of speech, said to raise them up.[60]

All slanderers are the devil's bellows to blow up contention, but those are the worse which blow at the back of the fire...He is a fool if not a knave who picks up stolen goods and harbors them; in slander as well as robbery, the receiver is as bad as the thief. If there were no gratified hearers of ill reports, there would be an end of the trade of spreading them. Trapp says, that the tale-bearer carrieth the devil in his tongue, and the tale-hearer carries the devil in his ear...The saints of God must not be light of hearing, much less of believing all tales, rumors, and reports of their brethren; and charity requireth that we do not only stop and stay them, but that we examine them before we believe them. "*Nor taketh up a reproach.*" The sin of being too ready to believe ill reports. Common, cruel, foolish, injurious, wicked.[61]

Exegesis and Application of the Passage

While Psalm 14 gives us a vivid description of the character of the wicked, Psalm 15 describes the character of the righteous. The righteous are viewed as people who desire above all other things in life to live in fellowship with God. Thus they "abide" in the tabernacle in the sense of being "at home" in the presence of God.

David lays out ten characteristics of a righteous man. The ancient rabbis saw a clear parallel with the Ten Commandments. Indeed, there are many parallels that could be drawn between the Ten Commandments and the Ten Characteristics. But, suffice it to say, the character of a righteous man conforms to the Law of God. Thus true righteousness is lawful, not antinomian.

This is something that professing Christians today have forgotten. They have little or no concern to conform their lives to the Law of God as revealed in Scripture. Instead, they look within themselves to their own reason, feelings, experience or faith as the Origin of truth, justice, morals, meaning, and beauty.

One element of a godly character focuses on how you use your tongue. This theme is later developed in the New Covenant Scriptures by James, the half brother of Jesus. The Old and New Testaments record how the tongue has been used to bless and to curse others. It has the power to heal and to wound.

The vast majority of charismatic Christians think that "holiness" consists of spectacular feats of spirituality such as healings, prophesying, speaking in tongues, holy laughter, etc. The vast majority of Reformed people are preoccupied with knowledge for knowledge's sake. They assume that holiness is determined by the amount of theology one knows. Thus the amount of knowledge you have determines the degree of holiness in your life. Being "mighty in intellect" does not necessarily mean you are "mighty in spirit." Just as knowledge without love is blind, love without knowledge is mere sentimentality.

The focus of our study is found in verses two and three. It is a Hebrew poetic parallel in which a righteous man is first described in three positive ways and then contrasted in three negative ways.

First, a godly man "walks in integrity," i.e. he holds fast to his moral principles and does not compromise, retreat, give way, or sell out to the highest bidder. He will keep his inner moral compass regardless if everyone else has gone astray. "Standing alone" in the face of the temptation to go along with the crowd is a rare virtue today.

Second, he "works righteousness," i.e. the end result of his words and works is to increase righteousness in the lives of those around him. He not only practices righteousness in his own life, he also promotes the practice of it in the lives of others. He wants to see Christians living in obedience to the Law and to see righteousness reigning in their hearts and homes. He desires to see churches submit to the Headship of Christ and to conform their doctrine and practices to His rule.

Third, "he speaks truth in his heart," i.e. he really desires to know the truth according to God's Word. He loves the truth and thus promotes it, defends it, rejoices over it, encourages it, and sows it like a farmer does seed.

David then gives us three things which a righteous man will **not** do:

> "walks in integrity" versus "does not slander with his tongue"
>
> "works righteousness" versus "does no evil to his neighbor"
>
> "speaks truth in his heart" versus "does not take up a reproach"

First, "he does not slander with his tongue," he does not accept, entertain, and then spread slander and gossip about others. You cannot "walk in integrity" and slander others at the same time. A godly man will not be a gossip monger or busy body who seeks out and delights in destroying the reputations and ministries of others.

Second, "he does no evil to his neighbor," i.e. he does not desire to harm his brothers and does not rejoice in evil. You cannot "work righteousness" and "do evil" at the same time.

Third, he "does not take up a reproach," he does not pick up and make his own the taunts and mocking of others. When person A offended person B, person B slandered A to C, D, E, F, etc. by mocking and reviling his character and motives. These people "took up" the slanders, slurs, gossip, evil speaking, taunts, mocking, ridicule, and reviling that B has launched against A.

It does not matter if the offense were valid or invalid, true or false. B was offended by something A did or said. But, instead of going to A in private to clarify and resolve the issue, B slandered A to others. Even though they may have never met A, they "take up" B's offense and attack A on the behalf of B. But, you cannot "speak truth in your heart" and "take up" other peoples' slanders and taunts. The sin of "taking up" the taunts, ridicules, cruel mocking, and slander of people is like picking up dog dung and smearing it on others.

Pro. 25:8-10 Do not rush out in public to argue your case because, in the end, what will you do when your neighbor puts you to shame publicly? Instead, argue your case with your neighbor in private, and do not reveal confidential matters to others lest those who hear you will publicly rebuke you, and an evil report about you will not soon pass away.

Commentaries:

The rabbis understood verse 9 as calling for discussion of the matter with one's neighbor. If the matter is settled in your favor, you're not to "betray a confidence" and tell everyone what your neighbor did wrong. Verse 10 shows that anyone who betrays confidences soon loses the trust of others to work out fair and private resolutions in the future. [62]

First, do not rush into public conflict, certain that right is on your side, nor if you make it a private matter, reveal all your sources; either way you may end up humiliated (8–10). Don't lose your self-control, or you may find you have lost everything (28). [63]

Ver. 9.—**Debate thy cause with thy neighbor himself** (Matt. 18:15; see on ver. 8). If you have any quarrel with a neighbor, or are drawn into a controversy with him, deal with him privately in a friendly manner. **And discover not a secret to another**; rather, *the secret of another*. Do not bring in a third party, or make use of anything entrusted to you by another person, or of which you have become privately informed, in order to support your cause. [64]

79

Our first desire is to "tell the whole world" and get everybody on our side. But the Bible counsels just the opposite: talk to the person alone and do not allow others to interfere. This is what Jesus commanded in Matt. 18:15–17, and if this policy were followed in families and churches, there would be fewer fights and splits. It is sad when professing Christians tell everybody but the one involved. Certainly, it takes courage and Christian love to talk over a difference with a brother or sister, but this is the way to grow spiritually and to glorify Christ. [65]

Perhaps the matter in variance is a secret, not fit to be divulged to any, much less to be brought upon the stage before the country; and therefore end it privately, that it may not be discovered." *Reveal not the secret of another,* so some read it. "Do not, in revenge, to disgrace thy adversary, disclose that which should be kept private and which does not at all belong to the cause." [66]

Argue your case with your neighbor himself: Argue your case in this context means to discuss differences of opinion, and with your neighbor himself means "privately." And do not disclose another's secret:

80

Disclose renders a word meaning "uncover" and refers to making something public, exposing it to the public, or telling others about it. A secret refers to information that one of the parties to the dispute has learned about the other. REB translates "Argue your own case with your neighbor, and do not reveal another's secrets." In some languages we may also say, for example, "Exchange words with your friend, but do not tell others what you have learned about him." A translation in a Pacific language says: "If you and your neighbor have a row about something, it is best for just you-two to sort it out, and afterwards you must not talk about this private business." [67]

A courtier should not betray confidences. In an argument with a neighbor the temptation exists to reveal secret information about him. A person who betrays confidential information will be reviled as a talebearer by those who hear him. His bad reputation would remain with him forever (25:9–10). [68]

Debate thy cause with thy neighbor himself (Matt. 18:15; see on ver. 8). If you have any quarrel with a neighbor, or are drawn into a controversy with him, deal with him privately in a friendly manner. And discover not a secret to another; rather, the secret of another. Do not bring in a third party, or make use of anything entrusted to you by another person, or of which you have become privately informed, in order to support your cause. Ver. 10.—Lest he that heareth it put thee to shame; i. e. lest anyone, not the offended neighbor only, who hears how treacherous you have been, makes your proceeding known and cries shame upon you. [69]

The considerate Christian will rather concede rights, than insist upon them to the hazard of his own soul, and to the injury of the Church. (1 Cor. Vi.1-7). Hasty strife must always be wrong. Think well beforehand, whether the case be right, or even if it be, whether it worth the contention. Duly calculate the uncertainty or conse-quence of the end... How many unholy heats would be restrained by the practice of these rules of wisdom and love! [70]

Exegesis and Application of the Passage

The Book of Proverbs is the passage of full mention on how to live a righteous life by practicing wisdom in everyday affairs. The Jewish view of wisdom is in stark contrast to the

Greek conception. The Greeks loved to talk about "wisdom" in the abstract while living lives of immorality and greed.

In contrast, the Hebrews understood that "wisdom" is looking at life from God's perspective as revealed in Scripture and "understanding" is solving daily problems with divine wisdom. Wisdom is thus the *skill* of living life according to Torah.

It is thus no surprise that Proverbs devotes so much time on how to handle disagreements, strife, slander, gossip, accusations, contention, etc. There is nothing more painful than a breach of fellowship with long time friends or family members.

In Pro. 25:8-10, Solomon warns that it is not wise to rush out and publicly accuse your neighbor of evil because when he hears about it, he may refute what you say and you will end up not only with egg on your face but you will also end up with the reputation of being a talebearer, slanderer, and gossip monger.

Instead of going on the internet and attacking people, it would be *wise* to go to people in private and resolve those issues. Those who immediately go on the internet and trash the character and motives of people often claim to base their accusations on "secret" information about their enemies. Yet, Solomon warns us that to reveal such "secrets" is not a virtue but a *vice*.

It is never right to reveal what is essentially private and confidential. For example, a woman going through a divorce made three internet videos ridiculing her husband's physical dimensions and performance in bed. Millions of people watched the videos and joined her in mocking her husband. This is exactly what Proverbs condemns.

While the Biblical Prophets mocked unbelief and rebellion against God as foolishness (Psa. 14:1), they did not mock and ridicule *people* for their physical appearance or poor health. They were not mean-spirited, vindictive or malicious. Their intent was not to hurt and wound others. They were not motivated by hatred or by a bitter, unforgiving spirit.

What can we say about so-called Christians who ridicule and mock Christian leaders and their ministries on the internet? Mocking, ridiculing, and reviling others are all condemned in Scripture as wicked (Pro. 17:5; 30:17; Isa. 51:7; 1 Cor. 5:11; 6:10; 2 Tim. 3:2). Jesus, the prophets, and apostles were cruelly mocked, reviled, taunted, and ridiculed (Matt. 27:29, 31; Heb. 11:36). When Elijah was mocked because he was bald, God's punishment was severe (2 Kings 2:23-24).

Matt. 18:15-22 Moreover, if your brother shall **trespass against you**, go and tell him his **fault** between you and him **alone**: if he shall hear you, you have gained your brother.

But if he will not hear you, *then* take with you one or two more brothers, that by the mouth of two or three eye witnesses every word may be established.

And if he shall neglect to hear them, tell *it* unto the church:

But if he neglects to hear the church, let him be to you as a heathen man and a publican.

Then came Peter to him, and said, "Lord, how often shall my brother **sin against me**, and I forgive him? Until seven times?" Jesus said unto him, "I say not unto you, "Until seven times," but, "Until seventy times seven."

Commentaries:

> *Keep the matter private.* Approach the person who sinned and speak with him alone. It is possible that he does not even realize what he has done. Or, even if he did it deliberately, your own attitude of submission and

love will help him to repent and apologize. Above all else, go to him with the idea of winning your brother, not winning an argument. It is possible to win the argument and lose your brother. We must have a spirit of meekness and gentleness when we seek to restore a brother or sister (Gal. 6:1). We must not go about condemning the offender, or spreading gossip. We must lovingly seek to help him in the same way we would want him to help us if the situation were reversed. The word *restore* in Galatians 6:1 is a Greek medical word that means "to set a broken bone." Think of the patience and tenderness that requires! [71]

The aim must be to win your brother over, restora-tion, not punishment. To that end, the minimum of publicity must be used. The erring brother must be approached alone. [72]

If the matter can be settled at that level, there is no need for it to go any further. [73]

It is necessary to note, however, that only a real sin is referred to, one that is apparent as such when one or two other brethren are called in on the case and when the whole congregation considers the matter. This excludes what a sensitive brother may deem a sin without due warrant that is as such. The context furthermore supplies the directive that the sin is of such nature that I cannot be permitted to pass as a weakness and fault such as we all commit, sometimes daily. "Between thee and him alone," enjoins strict privacy and forbids blurting out the matter in public, or spreading it in secret by telling one or the other, or at once lodging complaint before the church authorities. This direction intends to shield the sinning brother and is prompted by love. It also makes it as easy as possible to confess the sin and to ask for pardon.

The motive Jesus desires to find operative in his heart is love toward the sinning brother, the true, spiritual love that desires to assert no rights of its own but only to gain the brother by freeing him from his sins. [74]

To spare the honor of the brother who has Sinned Jesus adds that such an interview with the offender must take place "while you are alone with him," literally, "between you and him alone," that is, privately. There must be a tête-à-tête, a brotherly "face-to-face" confron-tation. [75]

The person who is offended must go to the person offending (who may not even realize a wrong has been done) and talk about the problem (18:15). [76]

First, Neither harbor a grudge against your offending brother, nor break forth upon him in presence of the unbelieving; but take him aside, show him his fault, and if he own and make reparation for it, you have done more service to him than even justice to yourself. Next, If this fail, take two or three to witness how just your complaint is, and how brotherly your spirit in dealing with him. Again, If this fail, bring him before the Church or congregation to which both belong. Lastly, If even this fail, regard him as no longer a brother Christian, but as one "without"— as the Jews did Gentiles and publicans. [77]

What should we do when another Christian has sinned against us or caused us to stumble? Our Lord gave several instructions. Keep the matter private. Approach the person who sinned and speak with him alone. It is possible that he does not even realize what he has done. Or, even if he did it deliberately, your own attitude of submission and love will help him to repent

87

and apologize. Above all else, go to him with the idea of winning your brother, not winning an argument. It is possible to win the argument and lose your brother. We must have a spirit of meekness and gentleness when we seek to restore a brother or sister (Gal. 6:1). We must not go about condemning the offender, or spreading gossip. We must lovingly seek to help him in the same way we would want him to help us if the situation were reversed. The word restore in Galatians 6:1 is a Greek medical word that means "to set a broken bone." Think of the patience and tenderness that requires!

Ask for help from others. If the offender refuses to make things right, then we may feel free to share the burden with one or two dependable believers. We should share the facts as we see them and ask the brethren for their prayerful counsel. After all, it may be that we are wrong. If the brethren feel the cause is right, then together we can go to the offender and try once again to win him. Not only can these men assist in prayer and persuasion, but they can be witnesses to the church of the truth of the conversation (Deut. 19:15; 2 Cor. 13:1).

When sin is not dealt with honestly, it always spreads. Ask the church for help. Remember, our goal is not the winning of a case but the winning of a brother. The word gained in Matthew 18:15 is used in 1 Corinthians 9:19–22 to refer to winning the lost; but it is also important to win the saved. This is our Lord's second mention of the church (see Matt. 16:18), and here it has the meaning of a local assembly of believers. [78]

As the greater part of men are driven by ambition to publish with excessive eagerness the faults of their brethren, Christ seasonably meets this fault buy enjoining us to cover the faults of brethren, as far as lies in our power; for those who take pleasure in the disgrace and infamy of brethren are unquestionably carried away by hatred and malice, since, if they were under the influence of charity, they would endeavor to prevent the shame of their brethren.

…Moses forbids sentence to be pronounced on a matter that is unknown, and defines this to be the lawful mode of proving, that it be established by the testimony of two or three witnesses. [79]

Exegesis and Application of the Passage

Matt. 18:15-22 is an illustration of the low level of biblical knowledge today.

1. The liberals deny that Jesus spoke these words and claim that it is an interpolation made by later redactors. The earliest copy of Matthew is dated around A.D. 65 and it has the passage in the text. No later manuscripts of Matthew omit the passage. Thus there is no textual evidence whatsoever that it was a later interpolation.

2. Some Dispensationalists claim that the passage applies only to the Jewish synagogue and thus does not apply to the church because it did not exist until Pentecost. Thus Christians need not obey it. But they are inconsistent in their hermeneutic and have no problem seeing the Lord's Supper and the Great Commission belonging to the church, even though they were given before Pentecost.

    > To hold that Christ would announce that He was going to build His "church" and one chapter later not refer to the New Testament church when He uses the same term "church," but is referring to something else, is to fly in the face of all reasonable exegesis. It is clear that Christ was referring to His church in contrast to the Jews' church. Thus the context from chapter 16 to our passages is in favor of a congregational interpretation of the term "church." [80]

3. Some Reformed scholars believe that the word "church" as in "tell it to the church" refers to the

synagogue, not the church. Thus the passage does not directly relate to Christians. The same inconsistency is present as found in the dispensational exegesis.

4. Most "Christians" today simply ignore the passage entirely and violate it without any regard to what Jesus commanded. When they are upset with someone, they do not go to him or her in private but immediately slander the person to others and gossip about them behind his or her back. They are thus guilty of being "slanderers," and "back-biters."

   They cloak their slander by pretending it is only "prayer requests" and speak of it in terms of "concerns." They rationalize, "I cannot go to the person because he would not listen," "I am afraid of him," "It will not work," etc.

   They often use the internet to broadcast their accusations and even ridicule, mock, and taunt their victims without mercy. They attack his family, friends, church, business, and anyone who dares defend them against their slander. They do not have any conscience and will make up lies at will.

5. A few well-meaning Christians today attempt to follow the passage but do not understand what it says.

   a. Some Christians assume that Matt. 18:15-22 should be applied to any offense made by anyone at anytime to anyone. They become involved with offenses that supposedly happened to someone else and become a "busybody" by "taking up the offense" from someone else and making it their own. They then go after someone who never did anything to them. But this is a sin according to Psa. 15:3.

b. Some Christians assume that Matt. 18 concerns any offense no matter how little. They assume that having their feelings hurt is a sin. For example, one day in church, a member failed to say "Hello" when passing a man in the hall. The man was offended because the member did not say "Hello." He stewed over the issue until he became very angry because he had been "disrespected." Following his misunderstanding of Mathew 18, he went to the member in private, rebuked him for the "sin" of not saying "Hello," and demanded repentance. The member refused to admit that he had sinned by not saying "Hello" and did not ask for forgiveness. He thought the man was being an idiot and told him so.

The man now complained to two or three friends who "took up" his offense and became angry at the member. They went to the member and demanded repentance. But he refused to admit his "sin" of not saying "Hello" and refused to ask for forgiveness. He told them that they were "making mountains out of mole hills."

The angry group now went to the pastor and demanded that church discipline be done on the member. They wanted him excommunicated from the church for not saying "Hello!"

The pastor talked with the man and found that he had been preoccupied with a personal problem that day and did not hear the man say "Hello." As the pastor prayed about what to do, he asked himself, "Where in the Bible do we find the "sin" of not saying 'Hello'? Nowhere! Does this "sin" merit church discipline?" No!

The pastor admonished the group for misapplying Matt. 18 and warned them that they manifested an anger and bitter spirit of vengeance. The witnesses had committed the sin of taking up offense and the offended brother was indeed "making a mountain out of a mole hill." Love should cover those kinds of small offenses.

The group was enraged against the pastor and set up blogs on the internet to attack him for the sin of failing to follow Matt. 18! They vented their anger against the pastor, his wife, and children.

What they failed to understand is that there are two kinds of sins listed in the Bible. There are those sins that are consistent with a profession of faith because they are part of the ongoing struggle of sanctification that all Christians experience (James 3:2). For example, we all struggle with pride. Such sins are never viewed in the Bible as liable for church discipline. If church discipline were to be done for pride or lust, there would be no one left in the church!

But, there are also sins that are not-consistent with a profession of faith and those who make a practice of those sins are liable for church discipline (ex. 1 Cor. 6:9-10).

Matt. 18 is part of the process of church discipline and has in view sins and transgressions that are *inconsistent* with a profession of faith. It was never intended to suggest that people be excommunicated for any offense whatsoever.

Matt. 18 thus does not apply to *minor* personal offenses, hurt feelings, bruised egos, or wounded pride. Jesus had in view real "sins" and "transgressions" condemned in Scripture. If the "offense" was not a sin according to Scripture, Matt. 18 did not apply.

c. We must also point out that Matt. 18 has in focus people who attend the *same* church and are under the authority of the *same* elders. The process will not work when the people involved are members of different churches.

A pastor had a friend who was put under discipline for sin by the church he attended. This pastor foolishly assumed that he could force himself on that church and make them take away the discipline of his friend. When they rejected his attempt to interfere with the internal operations of their church, he started a smear campaign against the pastor—although he did not personally know the man. He was a "busybody" and a "meddler" according to Scripture.

d. The last court of appeal is the local congregation. There is no group or individual above the local church who is given authority to adjudicate or arbitrate issues within that church. Lenski comments,

> The Church (congregation) is thus the final court of appeal. Those who would place above it a still higher authority: the pope, a bishop, some church board,

a house of bishops, a synod composed of clerics or these combined with lay delegates, go beyond the Word of Christ and the teachings of the apostles. In a difficult case the local congregation may seek counsel or advice, but the final jurisdiction in regard to a sinning member belongs to the congregation alone and no one ought either by direct or indirect means to nullify that jurisdiction. [81]

e.   The passage clearly assumes that when someone is put under church discipline, other churches should honor it. But, today, someone under discipline can simply walk across the street to another church and the pastor not only receives him with open arms but attacks the church that put him under discipline!

f.   Ministerial associations should take special heed to this biblical principle. One "fellowship" of pastors interfered with the internal business affairs of a member church. Even though they had *no biblical warrant* to judge the employer/employee decisions of that independent church, they condemned the church for letting several employees go. When confronted by the pastor for violating Scripture and seeking to "lord it over" his church, they publicly attacked his motives and character. They were guilty of doing what they accused the pastor of doing: pastoral abuse.

6. The "**fault**" in view must be a "**trespass**," i.e. "**sin**." Thus the issue must be a sin *according to the Bible*. If you cannot find a verse in the Bible that calls what you are upset about a "sin," then it is only a personal offense and does not merit action. Personal offenses such as hurt feelings, embarrassment, etc. are not allowable. Judging the motives of the heart (1 Cor. 4:3-5) is forbidden by Scripture. Your feelings and personal opinion do not count.

7. The sin must be "**against you**," not someone else (v. 21 "against *me*"). You cannot go to someone because of what he supposedly did or said to someone else. To do so is the sin of taking up someone's offense (Psa. 15:3).

8. Once you see from Scripture (not your feelings or opinions) that someone has **sinned** against you, the **first step** is *to give him the benefit of the doubt by going to him in private to ask questions to see if you misunderstood him or did not hear him correctly.* You do **not** go to rebuke the first time you meet with someone, because you must **first find out if he actually did or said something that violated Scripture**. Love does not assume ill of people (1 Cor. 13:7).

9. When a **brother sins against** another, **the two of** them should discuss the matter. Going in private and finding out if you were sinned against by that person usually closes the issue, because we often misjudge others, and once we ask questions of clarification the issue often evaporates.

10. If you find that the person did in fact sin against you according to Scripture, then ask him to apologize to you for what he said or did. **If he does so, the issue is closed and should not be gossiped about to others.**

11. If the person refuses to apologize to you for sinning against you according to Scripture, then meet with him a **second** time, but this time **take two or three eyewitnesses** who will witness your request that he or she repent and seek forgiveness.

12. If the person refuses to repent in the presence of two or three eye witnesses, **then the issue should be taken to the "church."** This has always been understood as taking place in three phases: First, you ask the pastor or the elders of the church to investigate the sin in question. Second, if they find that the person has sinned according to the Bible, they will ask him to repent. Third, if he does not do so, then church discipline is to be done.

13. Peter followed up on this issue and asked **how many times should we forgive someone**? The rabbis said that three times was the limit of forgiveness. After the third time, you don't have to forgive someone. In order to outdo them, Peter suggested that we should forgive someone seven times. He thought this would impress the Lord and win some points from the other disciples. But Jesus replied that we should forgive people "seventy times seven," i.e. *as many times as they repent*!

Conclusion:

Matt. 18 is the biblical antidote to all the poisonous slander and gossip found on the internet. It lays out a three part procedure that begins with going to someone in private to clarify what was said or done. If this first step is not followed, it *invalidates* anything else that is done. If the offended person immediately goes public with his accusations, he is in sin. If a church or ministerial society receives accusations that were not first submitted to the person under review and goes public with those invalid accusations, they have sinned against the accused. The first step makes or breaks the process.

1 Tim. 5:17-21 Let the elders who rule well be given double honor, especially they who labor in the word and doctrine for the scripture says, "You shall not muzzle the ox that treads the corn." And, "The laborer *is* worthy of his reward." Do not entertain an accusation against an elder unless it is established on the testimony of two or three eye witnesses. Those elders who are convicted of sin should be rebuked before the entire congregation, in order that the other members of the church may fear. I charge you before God, and the Lord Jesus Christ, and the elect angels, that you observe these things without preferring one before another, doing nothing by partiality.

Commentaries:

> *Against an elder receive not an accusation, but before two or three witnesses.* Here is the scripture-method of proceeding against an elder, when accused of any crime. Observe,
>
> 1. There must be an accusation; it must not be a flying uncertain report, but an accusation, containing a certain charge, must be drawn up. Further, he is not to be proceeded against by way of enquiry; this is according to the modern practice of the inquisition, which draws up articles for men to purge themselves of such crimes, or else to accuse themselves; but, according to the advice of Paul, there must be an accusation brought against an elder.

2. This accusation is not to be received unless supported by two or three credible witnesses; and the accusation must be received before them, that is, the accused must have the accusers face to face, because the reputation of a minister is, in a particular manner, a tender thing; and therefore, before anything be done in the least to blemish that reputation, great care should be taken that the thing alleged against him be well proved, that he be not reproached upon an uncertain surmise; "but (v. 20) *those that sin rebuke before all;* that is, thou needest not be so tender of other people, but rebuke them publicly." Or "those that sin before all rebuke before all, that the plaster may be as wide as the wound, and that those who are in danger of sinning by the example of their fall may take warning by the rebuke given them for it, *that others also may fear.*"[82]

Paul was deeply aware of opposition to the ministry. He had already spoken of the need to guard the congregation from the reproach of slanderers (cf. 3:2, 7), and would do so again (6:1). Here he stipulated the procedure for separating valid accusations from false ones. It is the venerable approach of both the Old Testament (cf. Deut. 19:15) and the New (cf. Matt. 18:16; John 8:17; 2 Cor. 13:1), wherein an accusation should be considered only if two or three witnesses swear to it.

When such accusations would then prove to be true, Timothy was to rebuke the offenders publicly, that is, before the entire congregation. In this way the remaining members could take warning (lit., "have fear"). Fear of the discipline of God, in this case administered through the congregation, is a healthy thing in a Christian, especially for those in places of leadership. Modern congergations that ignore church discipline do so at the peril of both the offender and themselves. [83]

Paul's first caution to Timothy was to be sure of his facts, and the way to do that is to have witnesses (1 Tim. 5:19). This principle is also stated in Deuteronomy 19:15; Matthew 18:16; and 2 Corinthians 13:1. I think a dual application of the principle is suggested here.

First, those who make any accusation against a pastor must be able to support it with witnesses. Rumor and suspicion are not adequate grounds for discipline.

Second, when an accusation is made, witnesses ought to be present. In other words, the accused has the right to face his accuser in the presence of witnesses.

A church member approached me at a church dinner one evening, and began to accuse me of ruining the church. She had all sorts of miscellaneous bits of gossip, none of which were true. As soon as she started her tirade, I asked two of the officers standing nearby to witness what she was saying. Of course, she immediately stopped talking and marched defiantly away.

It is sad when churches disobey the Word and listen to rumors, lies, and gossip. Many a godly pastor has been defeated in his life and ministry in this way, and some have even resigned from the ministry. "Where there's smoke, there's fire" may be a good slogan for a volunteer fire department, but it does not apply to local churches. "Where there's smoke, there's fire" could possibly mean that somebody's tongue has been "set on fire of hell!" (James 3:6)

101

Paul's second caution was that Timothy do everything openly and aboveboard. The under-the-counter politics of city hall have no place in a church. "In secret have I said nothing," said Jesus (John 18:20). If an officer is guilty, then he should be rebuked before all the other leaders (1 Tim. 5:20). He should be given the opportunity to repent, and if he does he should be forgiven (2 Cor. 2:6–11). Once he is forgiven, the matter is settled and should never be brought up again.

Paul's third caution (1 Tim. 5:21) is that Timothy obey the Word no matter what his personal feelings might be. He should act without prejudice against or partiality for the accused officer. There are no seniority rights in a local church; each member has the same standing before God and His Word. To show either prejudice or partiality is to make the situation even worse.[84]

Timothy was not to be disturbed by unproved private complaints, but to give due weight to the rights of the presbyterial office, and to condemn no innocent man unheard. "It might easily happen, in a church so large and mixed as the Ephesian, that one or

102

another, from wounded feelings of honor, from mere partisanship, or some selfish motive, would seek to injure a presbyter, and drag him down from his influential position; and against this the precept of the Apostle was the best safeguard" (Matthies).[85]

A judicial conviction was not permitted in De 17:6; 19:15, except on the testimony of at least two or three witnesses (compare Mt 18:16; Jn. 8:17; 2 Co 13:1; 1 Jn 5:6, 7). But Timothy's entertaining an accusation against anyone is a different case, where the object was not judicially to punish, but to admonish: here he might ordinarily entertain it without the need of two or three witnesses; but not in the case of an elder, since the more earnest an elder was to convince gainsayers (Tit 1:9), the more exposed would he be to vexatious and false accusations. How important then was it that Timothy should not, without strong testimony, entertain a charge against presbyters, who should, in order to be efficient, be "blameless" (1 Ti 3:2; Tit 1:6). 1 Ti 5:21, 24 imply that Timothy had the power of judging in the Church. Doubtless he would not condemn any save on the testimony of two or three witnesses, but in ordinary cases he would cite them, as the law of Moses also allowed, though there was only one witness. But in the case of elders, he would require two or three witnesses before even citing them; for their character for innocence stands higher, and they are exposed to envy and calumny more than others. [86]

The two or three witnesses are to ensure some kind of protection against false accusation from a single individual. This advice follows the normal Jewish practice. Where evidence for malpractice is forthcoming it must be presented publicly, i.e. before the whole church. Paul again shows his concern for the reputation of the church. Discipline is not only for the benefit of the individual but to provide a warning for others. [87]

No accusation (5:19). Deuteronomy 19:15 insists even ordinary people be protected against charges brought by an individual. Why is this repeated here? The elders' public position makes them more vulnerable than others to hostility and false accusations. And if such a charge were believed, it would hinder their effectiveness. [88]

An accusation against an elder must be upon — that is, must be based upon the oral testimony of — two or three witnesses. Note that though of old any Israelite was safeguarded against indictment and sentencing unless two or three reliable witnesses testified against him (cf. Deut. 17:6; cf. Num. 35:30; and see N.T.C. on John 5:31; 8:14), here (I Tim. 5:19) presbyters are safeguarded even against having to answer a charge (cf. Ex. 23:1 in LXX), unless it be at once supported by two or three witnesses. Lacking such support, the accusation must not even be taken up or entertained. The reputation of the elder must not be unnecessarily damaged, and his work must not suffer unnecessary interruption.

20. Nevertheless, at times a charge against an elder will have sufficient support to be entertained, and will afterward even be sustained by the facts. What then? Says Paul: Those who do wrong you must rebuke in the presence of all, so that also the others may be filled with fear (literally: may have fear).

21. Now in the matters discussed in verses 19 and 20, and, in fact, in any matter touching the discipline of church-

leaders, one is easily influenced by purely subjective considerations. But this can spell ruin for the church and for all those concerned. Timothy, as apostolic delegate in the churches of Ephesus and vicinity, must not allow this to happen to him. Even today biased judges, ecclesiastical "machines," so-called "investigating – committees" manned by job-hunters, "buddy-ism," and the like can easily destroy a denomination. Corruption generally begins "at the summit." Church history furnishes many examples. The man in the pew does not know what happened "while he slept." When he wakes up — if he ever does! — it is generally too late.

Hence, absolute impartiality and unimpeachable honesty in all such matters are essential. It is for that reason that the charge which the apostle now lays on Timothy is so very grave. Everything is at stake! The church of the twentieth century may well take to heart these solemn words: I charge (you) in the sight of God and of Christ Jesus and of the elect angels that you observe these instructions without prejudice, doing nothing from partiality. [89]

106

Because those in positions of leadership are subject to scrutiny, criticism, and rumors, Paul cautions Timothy not to "accept" or "acknowledge" as correct (BAGD s.v. παραδέχομαι) an "accusation/charge (κατηγορία) against (κατά) an elder unless" there are the requisite witnesses. ἐκτὸς εἰ μή** (a combination of ἐκτός and εἰ μή; 1 Cor. 14:5; 15:2) is a double (pleonastic) form of negation in postclassical Greek (BAGD s.v. ἐκτός) and means "unless" or "except."

Paul is, therefore, reminding Timothy to follow the principle of Dt. 19:15 in church discipline. Jesus also applied this principle to church discipline in Mt. 18:16, where witnesses are said to be necessary "so that ... every fact [literally "word"] may be confirmed," the witnesses being invited to sit with two people who are seeking to settle a personal or private sin (cf. Mt. 18:15 [variant reading]; Lk. 17:3, 4) that the witnesses did not themselves see. [90]

After having commanded that salaries should be paid to pastors, he likewise instructs Timothy not to allow them to be assailed by calumnies, or loaded with any accusation but what is supported by sufficient proof. But it may be thought strange, that he represents, as peculiar to elders, a law which is common to all. God lays down, authoritatively, this law as applicable to all cases, that they shall be decided "by the mouth of two or three witnesses." (Deuteronomy 17:6; Matthew 18:16.) Why then does the Apostle protect elders alone by this privilege, as if it were peculiar to them, that their innocence shall be defended against false accusations?

I reply, this is a necessary remedy against the malice of men; for none are more liable to slanders and calumnies than godly teachers. Not only does it arise from the difficulty of their office, that sometimes they either sink under it, or stagger, or halt, or blunder, in consequence of which wicked men seize many occasions for finding fault with them; but there is this additional vexation, that, although they perform their duty correctly, so as not to commit any error whatever, they never escape a thousand censures. And this is the craftiness of Satan, to draw away the hearts of men from ministers, that instruction may gradually fall into contempt. Thus not only is wrong done to innocent persons, in having their reputation unjustly wounded, (which is exceedingly base in regard to those who hold so honorable a rank) but the authority of the sacred doctrine of God is diminished.

And this is what Satan, as I have said, chiefly labors to accomplish; for not only is the saying of Plato true in this instance, that "the multitude are malicious, and envy those who are above them," but the more earnestly any pastor strives to advance the kingdom of Christ, so much the more is he loaded with envy, and so much the fiercer are the assaults made on him. Not only so, but as soon as any charge against the ministers of the word has gone abroad, it is believed as fully as if they were already convicted. This is not merely owing to the higher degree of moral excellence which is demanded from them, but because almost all are tempted by Satan to excessive credulity, so that, without making any inquiry, they eagerly condemn their pastors, whose good name they ought rather to have defended.

On good grounds, therefore, Paul opposes so heinous iniquity, and forbids that elders shall be subjected to the slanders of

109

wicked men till they have been convicted by sufficient proof. We need not wonder, therefore, if they whose duty it is to reprove the faults of all, to oppose the wicked desires of all, and to restrain by their severity every person whom they see going astray, have many enemies. What, then, will be the consequence; if we shall listen indiscriminately to all the slanders that are spread abroad concerning them? [91]

An elder sometimes received the opposite of honor. Ill will and personal hate might trump up some charges against him. Timothy is not to receive an accusation against an elder so as to take further steps about it, make an investigation, hears even the accused elder regarding the accusation, except on the basis of two or three witnesses, The honor due to the office demands this protection, for even a charge of which an elder is acquitted nevertheless damages his office and his work to some degree. Paul's purpose is to have no case taken up in which the verdict will after all have to be acquittal; also, and in the very first place, to prevent anybody from bringing up such a case. This is to be a special safeguard that is to be thrown around the good name of the office and its incumbents in the interest of the church itself. [92]

Exegesis and Application of the Passage

Ninety nine percent of all church splits would be avoided if Christians would only obey this passage. For some reason, people assume they can accuse a pastor of anything they want and do not need to produce any proof whatsoever to support their accusations. Pastors are in this way attacked and maligned every day.

One ex-member under discipline for the sin of schism went around the congregation meeting with people in secret. His trick was to begin by saying, "You know that I am a good man, don't you?" People would be kind and agree that he was a good man. Then he told them, "Then you know I would not lie to you, right? Then will you promise not to contact the pastor or the church about the secrets I am going to share with you?" The fools agreed to blindly accept his word as true and promised not to contact the church about his accusations. They left the church without ever checking to see if the accusations were true. This is exactly what God condemns in 1 Tim. 5:19.

Paul's pastoral advice would protect him and his fellow elders from slander and gossip. To do this, he raised the bar of evidence when it came to accusations against pastors because none are so maligned and hated as men of God who rebuke and admonish sinners. Those who are rebuked will slander the pastor's character and motives in the hopes that by doing so they can escape personal accountability for their sin.

Paul tells Timothy that when he is approached by someone in the church who accuses a pastor of something, to follow the principles laid down in Deut. 19, Proverbs, and Matt. 18. Ask them if they have gone in private to the pastor giving him the benefit of the doubt that he may not be guilty. If they have not bothered to go to him in private with their accusations, then he must refuse to "listen" to them, "pay attention to," "investigate" them or "give any credence" whatsoever.

The gossipy fellowship of pastors referred to before was headed by a busybody pastor who did not follow these Scriptural guidelines. He did not care if the accusers had gone in private to the pastor they were slandering. He even put together and distributed pages of accusations from people who admittedly never went to the pastor in private with their accusations! Since the people making these accusations clearly violated dozens of Scripture, they were in sin and should have been rebuked by that pastor.

Note that the passage concerns biblically defined sins that affect the life of the church. This means you have to give "chapter and verse" to prove that what you are accusing a pastor of is a sin *according to the Bible*. You have to prove *from Scripture* that the pastor is clearly in sin.

A pastor's wife contacted me and explained that a delegation of women from her church were on the way to rebuke her for the sin of not keeping her house as clean and neat as they desired. I first pointed out that if these women were coming as a *group*, they had *already sinned* against her by gossiping about her behind her back. Had any of them gone to her in private? No. Second, where does Scripture call a messy house a *sin*? In some cultures, homes have a dirt floor! Third, where in Scripture is a messy house such a serious sin that church discipline is warranted? Nowhere!

One trick of slanderers is to quote the KJV translation of 1 Thess. 5:22, "Abstain from every appearance of evil." They then argue that the pastor did or said something that "gives the appearance of evil," i.e. he did or said something that "*looked*" bad or questionable in *their* eyes, thus he is in sin.

First, the KJV is in error on this verse. The NASB translates it as "abstain from every *form* of evil."

Second, the Greek text is clear that Paul was *not* talking about things that might or might not be evil or might have the "appearance" of evil. He was telling Timothy to avoid *real* evil regardless of what form it takes. For example, I used to take my children to a restaurant that had a game where dinosaurs would pop out of a box in front of them. They had a large rubber mallet and had to hit the head of a dinosaur whenever it popped up. In the same way, Paul was saying that whenever evil pops up, avoid it. Hendriksen comments,

> from every *form* (or *kind,* not *appearance* here) of evil *hold off* (ἀπέχεσθε).[93]

Vincent agrees.

> **Appearance** (εἴδους). As commonly explained, abstain from everything that even *looks like* evil. But the word signifies *form* or *kind.* Comp. L. 3:22; J. 5:37, and see nearly the same phrase in Joseph. *Ant.* x., 3, 1. It never has the sense of *semblance.* Moreover, it is impossible to abstain from everything that looks like evil. [94]

One pastor was accused of the "sin" of preaching from the Hebrew and Greek text because it had "the appearance of evil" in that it looked like pride and conceit to preach that way!

Another typical trick is to say, "Where there is smoke there is fire. Thus I must look into such accusations." I usually respond, "Yes, you are right. Where there is smoke there is fire. But what kind of fire? The fire that produces such accusations is the fire of hell (James 3:6). Why do you want to descend into the hell fire from which such devilish accusations spring?"

Conclusion

If churches and ministerial fellowships would only follow the biblical guidelines in Deut. 19, Psa. 15, Pro. 25, Matt. 18, and 1 Tim. 5, much mischief would be aborted and much pain avoided. It is nothing less than open rebellion against the Headship of Christ over the local church when people violate these clear biblical guidelines.

Chapter Four

The Book of Proverbs on Gossip and Slander

The purpose of the Book of Proverbs is to enable us to make wise choices that honor God and to live a godly and righteous life. Giving and listening to slander and gossip dishonor God, spiritually harm us, and hurt those around us. Proverbs never recommends slander and gossip as either godly or wise. There is no "ministry of gossip" or "spiritual gift of slander." Those who spend their time inventing and passing on slander and gossip are fools as well as wicked according to the wisest man who ever lived. Proverbs 1:1-8 tells us the purpose of the book.

> The proverbs of Solomon the son of David, king of Israel;
>
> To know wisdom and instruction;
>
> To perceive the words of understanding;
>
> To receive the instruction of wisdom, justice, and judgment, and equity;
>
> To give subtlety to the simple,
>
> To the young person knowledge and discretion.
>
> A wise person will hear, and will increase learning; and a person of understanding shall attain unto wise counsels:
>
> To understand a proverb,

and the interpretation; the words of the wise, and their dark sayings.

The fear of YHWH *is* the beginning of knowledge: but fools despise wisdom and instruction.

The following passages deal with the evil nature and result of slander and gossip. Only a "fool" would ignore them. The verses and the commentaries are so clear and specific, that we will refrain from making any personal comments.

1. **Pro. 3:29-30**

   Do not make evil schemes against your neighbor, since he dwells securely next to you. Do not accuse someone without just cause, i.e. if he has not personally done you any harm."

Commentaries:

Do not plan evil against your neighbor: Plan evil means to plot or scheme to do harm or injury. In some languages to **plan evil** is expressed as "Don't put it in your heart to do bad things against" or "Don't think up ways to harm." **For Who dwells trustingly beside you: Trustingly** renders the same word as translated "securely" by RSV in verse 23 and refers to the peace and safety in which the person lives while depending on the goodwill of those who live around him. Making evil plans against such people is to betray their confidence. FRCL says:

- Do not plan to do bad to your friend because he lives close to you in trust. We may also say, for example,

- Don't think up evil ways to hurt the person living nearby who puts his confidence in you.

A translation that places the negative command at the end of the verse says…

- The people of your group live close to you and think you are their friend. Don't think of doing wrong to them.

Do not contend with a man for no reason: Contend means to dispute or quarrel. **Man** translates the Hebrew 'adam and refers to anyone, not just a male. Note that NRSV has revised man to "anyone." **For no reason** translates an expression that was used in 1.17 to mean "in vain" or "for no purpose." As used here the sense is similar, that is, "without a cause or reason." CEV says it well in idiomatic English: "Don't argue just to be arguing."

When he has done you no harm: This clause restricts arguing to cases in which harm has resulted. In some languages it will be more natural to begin with this clause and say, for example, "If someone has done you no harm, do not argue with them. There is no cause to argue." GECL says "Don't argue needlessly with someone who has done you no harm."

"We must never design any hurt or harm to anybody (v. 29): '*Devise not evil against thy neighbor;* do not contrive how to do him an ill-turn undiscovered, to prejudice him in his body, goods, or good name, and the rather because *he dwells securely by thee,* and, having given thee no provocation, entertains no jealousy or suspicion of thee, and therefore is off his guard.' It is against the laws both of honor and friendship to do a man an ill-turn and give him no warning. *Cursed be he that smites his neighbor secretly.* It is a most base ungrateful thing, if our neighbors have a good opinion of us, that we will do them no harm, and we thence take advantage to cheat and injure them." We must not be quarrelsome and litigious (v. 30): "Do not *strive with a man without cause;* contend not for that which thou hast no title to; resent not that as a provocation which

118

peradventure was but an oversight. Never trouble thy neighbor with frivolous complaints and accusations, or vexatious law-suits, when either there is no harm done thee or none worth speaking of, or thou mightest right thyself in a friendly way."[95]

Ver. 30.—The meaning of the precept in this verse is clear. We are not to strive or quarrel with a man unless he has first given us offence. So Le Clerc, "Nisi injuriâ prior lacessiverit." The admonition is directed against those who, from spite, jealousy, or other reasons, "stir up strife all the day long" with those who are quiet and peaceable...LXX., μὴ φιλεχθήσῃς, "Do not exercise enmity." [96]

2. **Pro. 6:12-19**

A naughty person, i.e. a wicked person,

walks with a forward mouth.

winks with his eyes,

speaks with his feet,

teaches with his fingers;

Forwardness *is* in his heart,

he devises mischief continually;

he sows discord.

Therefore shall his calamity come suddenly; suddenly shall he be broken without remedy.

These six sins YHWH hates:

Yea, seven are an abomination unto him: a proud look, a lying tongue, hands that shed innocent blood, a heart that devises wicked imaginations, feet that be swift in running to mischief, a false witness *that* speaks lies, he that sows discord among brethren.

Commentaries:

The person who stirs up dissension is the concern of vs 12–15 and 16–19. The description in vs 12–14 comes to its climax with this phrase. In a numerical saying like vs 16–19 all seven items can be equally important, and all are of course seriously meant, but after vs 12–15 the real point in vs 16–19 must lie with the last one (cf. 30:18–19, 29–31). The two observations are that the person will pay for it (15) and that God especially loathes this behavior (16). With the use of eyes, tongue, mind and feet here, contrast the advice in 4:23–27.[97]

Making mischief between relations and neighbors, and using all wicked means possible, not only to alienate their affections one from another, but to irritate their passions one against another. The God of love and peace hates him that sows discord among brethren, for he delights in concord. Those that by tale-bearing and slandering, by carrying ill-natured stories, aggravating everything that is said and done, and suggesting jealousies and evil surmises, blow the coals of contention, are but preparing for themselves a fire of the same nature.[98]

One that utters lies as a false witness, literally, one that breathes lies. The same characterization of the false witness is found also in chap. 14:5, 25; 19:5, 9. As respects the arrangement in which the seven manifestations of treacherous dealing are enumerated in these verses, it does not perfectly correspond with the order observed in ver. 12–14. There the series is mouth, eyes, feet, fingers, heart, devising evil counsels, stirring up strifes; here it is eyes, tongue, hands, heart, feet, speaking lies, instigating strife. With reference to the organs which are named as the instruments in the first five forms of treacherous wickedness, in the second enumeration an order is adopted involving a regular descent (ver. 16–19, eyes, tongue, hands, etc.); the base disposition to stir up strife, or to let loose controversy (see rem. on ver. 14) in both cases ends the series. [99]

A false witness who breathes out lies: False witness is used in Psa. 27:12 of persons who tell lies in court against the psalmist. In that verse those liars are said to breathe out violence. Here they are said to breathe out lies. This expression may refer to the endless flow of their lies or to the ease with which they lie. See 14:5 for the same expression. It is often translated "telling lies in court." A man who sows discord among brothers: Man is supplied by RSV. NRSV has revised to say "one who ...." Sows discord is as in verse 14. Brothers need not be restricted in sense to literal brothers but may be taken to refer to people who have a close association, such as friends or family members. CEV says, "or stir up trouble in a family." [100]

Seventh, God hates those that "sow discord among brethren," i.e., friends, associates, members of the same circle. The words "among brethren" underscore the diabolical nature of this sin which destroys the harmony and unity of those who ought to live together in brotherly affection.

The implication is that God smiles on brotherly love and frowns on any who would disrupt it (6:19). [101]

In verses 14-15 six urgent commands are given to steer clear of the path of the wicked, and verses 16-17 state the reason for the urgency in verses 14-15. Wicked people are so taken up with evil that they are unable to sleep till they hurt someone (cf. 1:15-16). Sin is so much a part of them that it is like their food (bread and wine). [102]

He soweth discord (Hebrew, midyânîm (Keri) yshāllêākh); literally, he sends forth (i.e. excites) strife; or, as the margin, he casteth forth strife. The Keri reading midyânîm, for the Khetib mdânîm, is probably, as Hitzig suggests, derived from Gen. 37:36. The phrase occurs again as shĭllākh mdânîm in ver. 19, and as shĭllākh mâdôn in ch. 16:28 (cf. ch. 10:12). This is the culminating point in the character of the wicked man. He takes delight in breaking up friendship and in destroying concord among brethren (see ver. 19), and thus destroys one of the most essential elements for promoting individual happiness and the welfare of the community at large. This idea of the community is introduced into the LXX., which reads, "Such an one brings disturbance to the city (ὁ τοσοῦτος ταραχὰς συνίστησι πόλει)." The motive cause may be either malice or self-interest. [103]

3.   **Pro. 10:10-12**

He that winks with the eye causes sorrow:

but a prating fool shall fall.

The mouth of a righteous person is a well of life: but violence covers the mouth of the wicked.

Hatred stirs up controversies:

but love covers all sins.

Commentaries

(10:10). "Winks maliciously" is to spread gossip or to attack by innuendo. The pain caused by vindictive or disparaging remarks stands in contrast to the positive impact of words spoken by the righteous, which are "a fountain of life" (v. 11). See also v. 21, "The lips of the righteous nourish many." [104]

10:12.   Hatred results in dissension (cf. 6:14) because people who despise each other can hardly work or live together in peace. Love contributes toward peace because it covers or forgives the faults of others (cf. 17:9). It does not dwell on those faults (cf. 1 Cor. 13:5; James 5:20; 1 Peter 4:8). "Covers" is kāsâh, the same word rendered "overwhelms" in Proverbs 10:6, 11. A wicked one's words are covered over with violence, but a righteous person covers up wrongs by forgiving the wrongdoers. [105]

Here is, 1. The great mischief-maker, and that is malice. Even where there is no manifest occasion of strife, yet hatred seeks occasion and so stirs it up and does the devil's work. Those are the most spiteful ill-natured people that can be who take a pleasure in setting their neighbors together by the ears, by tale-bearing, evil surmises, and misrepresen-ttations, blowing up the sparks of contention, which had lain buried, into a flame, at which, with an unaccountable pleasure, they warm their hands. 2. The great peace-maker, and that is love, which covers all sins, that is, the offences among relations which occasion discord. Love, instead of proclaiming and aggravating the offence, conceals and extenuates it as far as it is capable of being concealed and extenuated. Love will excuse the offence which we give through mistake and unadvisedly; when we are able to say that there was no ill intended, but it was an oversight, and we love our friend notwithstanding, this covers it. It will also overlook the offence that is given us, and so cover it, and make the best of it: by this means strife is prevented, or, if begun, peace is recovered and restored quickly. The apostle quotes this, 1 Pt. 4:8. Love will cover a multitude of sins. [106]

Quarrelsomeness vs. amiability (10:12). "Hatred stirs up strifes," i.e., by focusing on faults, making mountains out of molehills, and questioning motives. Hatred keeps alive the old feeling of revenge, and seeks opportunities of satisfying it. On the other hand, "love covers all transgressions." Love puts shortcomings out of sight, enables one to overlook insults and wrongs (cf. 1 Pet 4:8). This proverb is probably intended as a comment on the last line of the previous proverb, and possibly also on v. 10. The reprehensible actions mentioned in those verses are here attributed to hatred and the desire to stir up strife. [107]

4.   **Pro. 10:18**

He that hides hatred with lying lips,

and he that utters a slander, is a fool.

Commentaries:

Each of verses 18-21 refers to some aspects of talking. The subject of hatred was introduced in verse 12, and in verse 18 another thought is added to the subject. When a person hates someone but tries not to show it he is often forced to lie. And hatred often leads to slandering the other who is despised. The second line in verse 18 begins with and rather than "but," to show that the two thoughts of hatred and slander are not opposites. Such lying and slandering, born out of hatred, characterize a fool. [108]

Observe here, Malice is folly and wickedness. 1. It is so when it is concealed by flattery and dissimulation: He is a fool, though he may think himself a politician, that hides hatred with lying lips, lest, if it break out, he should be ashamed before men and should lose the opportunity of gratifying his malice. Lying lips are bad enough of themselves, but have a peculiar malignity in them when they are made a cloak of maliciousness. But he is a fool who thinks to hide anything from

127

God. 2. It is no better when it is vented in spiteful and mischievous language: He that utters slander is a fool too, for God will sooner or later bring forth that righteousness as the light which he endeavours to cloud, and will find an expedient to roll the reproach away. [109]

He who spreadeth slander is a fool. The meaning of this 2d clause does not stand in the relation of an antithesis to the preceding, but that of a climax, adding a worse case to one not so bad. If one conceals his hatred within himself he becomes a malignant flatterer; but if he gives expression to it in slander, abuse and base detraction, then as a genuine fool he brings upon himself the greatest injury. [110]

He who utters slander is a fool: Slander refers to rumors or bad things said against someone. Note TEV "gossip." Fool is the same as used first in 1.22. [111]

5. **Pro. 11:9**

With his mouth the godless man destroys his neighbor, But through knowledge the righteous will be delivered.

Commentaries:

Here is, 1. Hypocrisy designing ill. It is not only the murderer with his sword, but the hypocrite with his mouth, that destroys his neighbour, decoying him into sin, or into mischief, by the specious pretences of kindness and good-will. Death and life are in the power of the tongue, but no tongue more fatal than the flattering tongue. 2. Honesty defeating the design and escaping the snare: Through knowledge of the devices of Satan shall the just be delivered from the snares which the hypocrite has laid for him; seducers shall not deceive the elect. By the knowledge of God, and the scriptures, and their own hearts, shall the just be delivered from those that lie in wait to deceive, and so to destroy, Rom. 16:18, 19. [112]

Integrity vs. slander (11:9). "With his mouth the godless person (lit., the polluted) destroys his neighbor." Such a person lacks any honor. He attacks his neighbor with false accusations and insinuations. The verse may refer specifically to courtroom action. In that case, the idea is that a godless person is unscrupulous with regard to evidence in order to win his case. On the other hand, "through knowledge shall the righteous be delivered." His integrity enables an innocent person to expose the lies of his adversary (11:9). [113]

6. **Pro. 11:11-13**

By the blessing of the upright a city is exalted,

But by the mouth of the wicked it is torn down.

He who despises his neighbor lacks sense,

But a man of understanding keeps silent.

He who goes about as a talebearer reveals secrets,

But he who is trustworthy conceals a matter.

Commentaries:

In these community relationships (v. 9-15), right and wrong talking is mentioned several times: in verses 9, 11-13. Anyone who derides (bûz, "to despise, belittle, hold in contempt"; cf. comments on bûz in 1:7b) his neighbor (cf. 14:21) lacks judgment (see comments on 6:32; 10:13). It simply makes no sense to slander (cf. 10:18) one who lives or works nearby. Since that makes for friction and dissension, it is wise to keep quiet (hold one's tongue; cf. 10:19) even if he does know something unpleasant about his neighbor. Divulging a secret by malicious gossip is a betrayal of trust (also stated in 20:19). "A gossip" is literally "one who goes about in slander." Gossiping is also condemned in 16:28; 18:8; 26:20, 22. [114]

I. Silence is here recommended as an instance of true friendship, and a preservative of it, and therefore an evidence, 1. Of wisdom: A man of understanding, that has rule over his own spirit, if he be provoked, holds his peace, that he may neither give vent to his passion nor kindle the passion of others by any opprobrious language or peevish reflections. 2. Of sincerity: He that is of a faithful spirit, that is true, not only to his own promise, but to the interest of his friend, conceals every matter which, if divulged, may turn to the prejudice of his neighbor. II. This prudent friendly concealment is here opposed to two very bad vices of the tongue: 1. Speaking scornfully of a man to his face: He that is void of wisdom discovers his folly by this; he despises his neighbor, calls him Raca, and Thou fool, upon the least provocation, and tramples upon him as not worthy to be set with the dogs of his flock. He undervalues himself who thus undervalues one that is made of the same mould. 2. Speaking spitefully of a man

131

behind his back: A tale-bearer, that carries all the stories he can pick up, true or false, from house to house, to make mischief and sow discord, reveals secrets which he has been entrusted with, and so breaks the laws, and forfeits all the privileges, of friendship and conversation. [115]

Four proverbs against talkativeness, a slanderous disposition, foolish counsel and thoughtless suretyship.—He that speaketh contemptuously of his neighbor.—This is the rendering here required to correspond with the antithesis in the second clause; comp. 14:21; 13:13. [The E. V. and HOLDEN invert this relation of subject and predicate, while DE W., K., N., S., and M. agree with our author in following the order of the original—A.]— Ver. 13. He that goeth about as a slanderer betrayeth secrets.— With this expression, "to go tattling, to go for slander," comp. Lev. 19: 16; Jer. 9:3. With the expression גָּלָה סוֹד, revelavit arcanum, "to reveal a secret," comp. 20:19; 5:9; Am. 3:7. That not this "babbler of secrets" is subject of the clause (HITZIG), but "he that goeth slandering," the parallel second clause makes evident, where with the "slanderer" is contrasted the faithful and reliable, and with the babbler the man who "concealeth the matter, i.e., the secret committed to him." Comp. Ecclesiasticus 27:16. [116]

14:21 is a proverb similarly beginning with לְרֵעֵהוּ בָּז , 13:13 is another beginning with לְדָבָר בָּז . From this one sees that לְ בּוּז (cf. לְ בָּזָה, Isa. 37:22) does not mean a speaking contemptuously in one's presence; as also from 6:30, that contemptuous treatment, which expresses itself not in mockery but in insult, is thus named; so that we do not possess a German [nor an English] expression which completely covers it. Whoever in a derisive or insulting manner, whether it be publicly or privately, degrades his neighbour, is unwise (חֲסַר־לֵב as pred., like 6:32); an intelligent man, on the contrary, keeps silent, keeps his judgment to himself, abstains from arrogant criticisms, for he knows that he is not infallible, that he is not acquainted with the heart, and he possesses too much self-knowledge to raise himself above his neighbour as a judge, and thinks that contemptuous rejection, unamiable, reckless condemnation, does no good, but on the contrary does evil on all sides.

133

Prov. 11:13. The tattler is called רָכִיל (intensive form of רְ'כֵל), from his going hither and thither. רָכִיל אַנְשֵׁי , Ezek. 22:9, are men given to tattling, backbiters; רָכִיל ה'וֹלֵךְ (cf. Lev. 19:16), one of the tattlers or backbiters goes, a divulger of the matter, a tell-tale. It is of such an one that the proverb speaks, that he reveals the secret (ס'וד, properly the being close together for the purpose of private intercourse, then that intercourse itself, vid., at Ps. 25:14); one has thus to be on his guard against confiding in him. On the contrary, a נֶאֱמַן־רוּחַ, firmus (fidus) spiritu, properly one who is established, or reflexively one who proves himself firm and true (vid., at Gen. 15:6), conceals a matter, keeps it back from the knowledge and power of another. Zöckler rightly concludes, in opposition to Hitzig, from the parallelism that the הולך רכיל is subject; the arrangement going before also shows that this is the "ground-word" (Ewald); in 20:19*a* the relation is reversed: the revealer of secrets is rightly named (cf. Sir. 27:16, ὁ ἀποκαλύπτων μυστήριά κ.τ.λ.).[117]

7. **Pro. 12:6**

The words of the wicked are to lie in wait for blood:

but the mouth of the upright shall deliver them.

Commentaries:

The dominant theme in the rest of ch. 12 is again the use of words, in particular the contrasting effect of good and bad words. Righteous, upright, wise, prudent, truthful, peacemaking, kind words issued in justice, deliverance, praise, profit, healing, joy, discretion, encouragement and in God's delight. Wicked, twisted, foolish, lying, malevolent, thoughtless, unrestrained or plotting words issue in deceit, in hurt to other people, in discredit and trouble to oneself and in God's abhorrence. It is wise to listen to advice but to ignore insults rather than vice versa (15–16); but also to be cautious in relations with others.[118]

In the foregoing verse the thoughts of the wicked and righteous were compared; here their words, and those are as the abundance of the heart is. 1. Wicked people speak mischief to their neighbours; and wicked indeed those are whose words are to lie in wait for blood; their tongues are swords to those that stand in their way, to good men whom they hate and persecute. See an instance, Luc. 20:20, 21:2. Good men speak help to their neighbours: The mouth of the upright is ready to be opened in the cause of those that are oppressed (ch. 31:8), to plead for them, to witness for them, and so to deliver them, particularly those whom the wicked lie in wait for. A man may sometimes do a very good work with one good word.[119]

The words of the wicked are to lie in wait—a lying in wait—for blood (see ch. 1:11). The wicked, by their lies, slanders, false accusations, etc., endanger men's lives, as Jezebel compassed Naboth's death by false witness (1 Kings 21:13). The mouth of the upright shall deliver them; i.e. the innocent whose blood the wicked seek. The good plead the cause of the oppressed, using their eloquence in their favour, as in the Apocryphal Story of Susannah, Daniel saved the accused woman from the slanders of the elders.[120]

The tongue should be used for right purposes: bringing peace (15:1, 26); giving wise reproof to the erring (25:12; 28:23); delivering lost souls from death

(11:9; 14:3–5, 25; 12:6); teaching people the things of the Lord (15:7; 16:21, 23; 20:15); and carrying the good news of the Gospel (25:25). But Satan and the flesh want to control the tongue, and the results are sad. Perhaps more damage is done to lives, homes, and churches by the tongue than by any other means. It is sobering to realize that the tongue can be used to damage reputations and cause trouble, when it ought to be used to praise God, pray, and witness to others about Christ. The tongue is a "little member" of the body (James 3:5), but it is one member that must be yielded to God as a tool of righteousness (Rom. 6:12–13). Perhaps if we consider some of the sins of the tongue, it might encourage us to use our gift of speech more carefully.[121]

8. **Pro. 12:17-22**

The person who speaks the truth shows forth righteousness: but a false witness shows forth deceit.

There are those whose speech is like the piercings of a sword: but the tongue of the wise brings health.

The lip of truth shall be established forever: but a lying tongue is but for a moment.

Deceit is in the heart of them that imagine evil: but to the counselors of peace is joy.

There shall no evil happen to the just: but the wicked shall be filled with mischief.

Lying lips are abomination to YHWH: but they that deal truly are his delight.

A prudent man conceals knowledge: but the heart of fools proclaims foolishness.

Commentaries:

The Speech of Fools (12:16–22)

The proverbs which follow enumerate five types of foolish speech.

1. Angry speech (12:16). "A fool shows his annoyance in the same day." He shows that he is upset immediately. He has no idea of controlling himself or checking the expression of his wounded ego. Lashing out in the heat of anger, he arouses contention. On the other hand, "a prudent person conceals shame." He does not make a fool out of

himself by shooting off his mouth. He exercises restraint and ignores an insult. He knows that by showing his resentment he will only make matters worse. He knows that it is best to let passions cool before he attempts to set things right.

2. Perjured speech (12:17). "He that breathes (yaphiach) out truth utters righteousness." The verse relates to the testimony of a witness in a court of law. The term "righteousness" here is used in its legal sense of "justice." The idea is that a true witness supports the cause of justice by contributing to a right verdict. On the other hand, "a witness of lies [breathes out] deceit." Such a one misleads the judges and is responsible for a miscarriage of justice. By his perverted testimony he reveals his true character.

3. Inflammatory speech (12:18). "There is one who speaks thoughtlessly like the piercings of a sword." Reckless words often have a harmful, and even fatal, consequence. The edge of the sword was called "its

mouth." The human mouth can do as much damage as that "mouth" of metal. On the other hand, "the tongue of the wise is health." His words soothe anguish, undo injury, and heal wounds.

4. Deceitful speech (12:19). "The lip of truth shall be established forever." Truth is consistent and invincible. It endures the test of time. On the other hand, "a lying tongue is but for a moment." Literally, it lasts "while I wink the eye," i.e., lasts as long as it takes to blink an eye. Lying is soon found out and punished.

5. Evil counsel (12:20–22). "Deceit is in the heart of them that devise evil." The reference is to those who give evil advice. Such are treacherous counselors. Their advice can only bring misfortune, not joy and comfort.[122]

Moses warned about this sin in Lev. 19:16. A "talebearer" is one who runs from person to person telling matters that ought to be concealed, whether they are true or false. See 11:13. "Love covers all sins," says 10:12. See also 17:9, 1 Peter 4:8, and James

5:20. When we love others, we seek to help them privately, and we try to win them back to the right way (Matt. 18:15–18). Think how many people have been wounded by the talebearer. Words can be as deadly as weapons; in 25:18 Solomon compares deceitful words to three different weapons: a maul (battle-ax) that crushes at close range; a sword that cuts; and an arrow that pierces and can be shot from a distance. Stay away from the talebearer (20:19). He or she is a kindler of fires (26:20) and a destroyer of friendships (17:9).

The tongue is death or life, poison or medicine, as it is used. 1. There are words that are cutting and killing, that are like the piercings of a sword. Opprobrious words grieve the spirits of those to whom they are spoken, and cut them to the heart. Slanders, like a sword, wound the reputation of those of whom they are uttered, and perhaps incurably. Whisperings and evil surmises, like a sword, divide and cut asunder the bonds of love and friendship, and separate those that have been dearest to each other. 2. There are words that are curing and healing: The tongue of the wise is

141

health, closing up those wounds which the backbiting tongue had given, making all whole again, restoring peace, and accommo-dating matters in variance and persuading to reconci-liation. Wisdom will find out proper remedies against the mischiefs that are made by detraction and evil-speaking. [123]

9. **Pro. 14:5-7**

A faithful witness will not lie: but a false witness will constantly lie.

A mocker claims to seek wisdom, but will not find it: but knowledge is easy to find for those who are under-standing.

Escape from the presence of a foolish man, when you perceive that the lips of knowledge are not in him.

Commentaries:

It is unusual to read in Proverbs that a mocker (see comments on 13:1) seeks wisdom, but this shows that lack of desire is not his problem so much as lack of meeting the primary condition, fearing the Lord (1:7; 9:10). Apparently mockers look for wisdom in the wrong places. Knowledge is easily acquired by people who have discernment in spiritual things. They know where to look for true knowledge.

14:7. Verses 7-9 all include statements about fools. Verse 7 is the first imperative statement in the section beginning with 10:1. Also 14:7 is written in synthetic parallelism for the second line explains the first line. Since one's associations can influence him for good or bad (cf. 13:20), he ought to steer clear of being with the foolish (kesîl) for they speak without knowledge. They cannot offer the young anything of value. [124]

utter lies—or, "breathe out lies"—that is, habitually lies (Pr 6:19; compare Ac 9:1). Or the sense is, that habitual truthfulness, or lying, will be evidenced in witness-bearing. [125]

1. The reason why some people seek wisdom, and do not find it, is because they do not seek it from a right principle and in a right manner. They are scorners, and it is in scorn that they ask instruction, that they may ridicule what is told them and may cavil at it. Many put questions to Christ, tempting him, and that they might have whereof to accuse him, but they were never the wiser. No marvel if those who seek wisdom, as

Simon Magus sought the gifts of the Holy Ghost, to serve their pride and covetous-ness, do not find it, for they seek amiss. Herod desired to see a miracle, but he was a scorner, and therefore it was denied him, Lu. 23:8. Scorners speed not in prayer. 2. To those who understand aright, who depart from evil (for that is understanding), the knowledge of God and of his will is easy. The parables which harden scorners in their scorning, and make divine things more difficult to them, enlighten those who are willing to learn, and make the same things more plain, and intelligible, and familiar to them, Mt. 13:11, 15, 16. The same word which to the scornful is a savour of death unto death to the humble and serious is a savour of life unto life. He that understands, so as to depart from evil (for that is understanding), to quit his prejudices, to lay aside all corrupt dispositions and affections, will easily apprehend instruction and receive the impressions of it.

Verse 7

See here, 1. How we may discern a fool and discover him, a wicked man, for he is a foolish man. If we perceive not in him the lips of knowledge, if we find there is no relish or savour of piety in his discourse, that his communication is all corrupt and corrupting, and nothing in it good and to the use of edifying, we may conclude the treasure is bad. 2. How we must decline such a one and depart from him: Go from his presence, for thou perceivest there is no good to be gotten by his company, but danger of getting hurt by it. Sometimes the only way we have of reproving wicked discourse and witnessing against it is by leaving the company and going out of the hearing of it. [126]

10. **Pro. 14:15**

The naïve person believes every word he hears: but the wise person investigates carefully before taking action.

Commentaries:

The simple (peṯî, "naive, gullible"; see comments on 1:4) are easily influenced (see, e.g., 7:7-10, 21-23), but the prudent ('ārûm; cf. 14:8, 18 and see comments on 12:23) think before they act.[127]

It is folly to be credulous, to heed every flying report, to give ear to every man's story, though ever so improbable, to take things upon trust from common

145

fame, to depend upon every man's profession of friendship and give credit to everyone that will promise payment; those are simple who thus believe every word, forgetting that all men, in some sense, are liars in comparison with God, all whose words we are to believe with an implicit faith, for he cannot lie. 2. It is wisdom to be cautious: The prudent man will try before he trusts, will weigh both the credibility of the witness and the probability of the testimony, and then give judgment as the thing appears or suspend his judgment till it appears. Prove all things, and believe not every spirit.[128]

Verses 15–18 contrast wise and foolish people.

The simple believes everything: For simple see 1.4. This word in Hebrew is singular but may be expressed in the plural. Believes means to accept some thing as true or real. Everything renders a phrase meaning "every word" and probably means here that the simple person accepts as true everything he hears. Such a person lacks the maturity to distinguish between what is true and what is false. FRCL says "A naive person believes everything anyone tells him."

But the prudent looks where he is going is literally "but the prudent watches his steps." Note TEV. This line contrasts the prudent ("wise," "clever") person with the simple (naive) person in line 1. "Watches his steps" is a figure that means to be cautious, alert, or aware, with the sense of being careful not to be misled by untruth. In some languages this line is expressed, for example, "but the clever person keeps an eye on the path" or "if you are smart you sleep with one eye open." [129]

The credulous fool believes all that he hears without proof or examination; having no fixed principles of his own, he is at the mercy of any adviser, and is easily led astray. Eccles. 19:4, "He that is hasty to give credit is light-minded, and he that sinneth (thus) shall offend against his own soul." [130]

11. Pro. 15:1-4

A gentle answer will avoid anger: but a harsh answer will stir it up.

The tongue of the wise uses knowledge correctly: but the mouth of fools pours out foolishness.

The eyes of YHWH are in every place,

beholding the evil and the good.

A healing tongue is like a tree of life: but a perverse tongue is like a breach in the spirit.

Commentaries:

Words can encourage or depress an individual. Words that bring healing, that contribute to a person's emotional health, are like a tree of life (cf. 3:18; 11:30; 13:12), a source of strength and growth. Words that are deceitful (selep, "subversive"; used in the OT only here and in 11:3, "duplicity") can crush the spirit (cf. 15:13; 17:22; 18:14), or depress one's morale. [131]

A soft answer turns away wrath: Soft in relation to speech means "gentle," "kind," or, as REB says, "mild." It is a response without anger or harshness. The impor-tance of kindness and respect in the use of speech is expressed again in 24:26 and 25:15. Answer in this context refers to a response or reply to what someone, perhaps in anger, has said. Turns away translates the causative form of a verb meaning "to turn back." The thought is that the anger of the first speaker can be set aside or

148

calmed by a gentle response. Wrath is anger or fury. CEV says "A kind answer soothes angry feelings," and SPCL has "A friendly reply calms anger." In some languages it may be necessary to expand this line to say, for example, "Reply to a person with gentle words and you will calm their anger."

But a harsh word stirs up anger: A harsh word is literally "a word of pain," that is, one that causes pain, and the expression refers to a word or utterance spoken sharply or heatedly. Stirs up or "excites" contrasts with turns away in the first line. The verb refers to causing something to rise, in this case the angry emotions of the other speaker, as REB says: "but a sharp word makes tempers rise." GECL translates this full saying "A reconciling answer cools down anger, but a hurtful word heats it up."[132]

A good tongue is healing, healing to wounded consciences by comforting them, to sin-sick souls by convincing them, to peace and love when it is broken by accommodating differences, compromising matters in variance, and reconciling parties at variance; this is the healing of the tongue, which is a tree of life, the leaves of which have a sanative virtue, Rev. 22:2. He that knows how to discourse will make the place he lives in a paradise. 2. An evil tongue is wounding (perverseness, passion, falsehood, and filthiness there, are a breach in the spirit); it wounds the conscience of the evil speaker, and occasions either guilt or grief to the hearers, and both are to be reckoned breaches in the spirit. Hard words indeed break no bones, but many a heart has been broken by them. [133]

A gentle tongue is a tree of life: A gentle tongue is literally "a healing tongue." The thought expressed here is essentially the same as "a soft answer" in verse 1. The sense is "kind or comforting words." A tree of life, first used in 3:18, may be expressed as a simile, "like a tree that gives life" or, as in TEV, "... bring life." FRCL says "... is a source of life." But perverseness in it breaks the spirit: Perverseness renders a word meaning "twisted" or "crooked," as in 11:3 where "crookedness" is used. Something that is twisted is untrue or false. Perverseness parallels and contrasts the gentle tongue, not the tree of life. In other words false speech or lying

150

breaks the spirit, an expression that means "causes despair" or "leads to ruin." CEV translates "Kind words are good medicine, but deceitful words can really hurt."[134]

12. **Pro. 16:27-28**

A scoundrel loves to plot evil:

and in his lips there is burning fire.

A perverse person loves to stir up trouble:

and a gossiper separates best friends.

Commentaries:

There are those that are not only vicious themselves, but spiteful and mischievous to others, and they are the worst of men; two sorts of such are here described: 1. Such as envy a man the honor of his good name, and do all they can to blast that by calumnies and misrepresent-tations: They dig up evil; they take a great deal of pains to find out something or other on which to ground a slander, or which may give some color to it. If none appear above ground, rather than want it they will dig for it, by diving into what is secret, or looking a great way back, or by evil suspicions and surmises, and forced innuendos. In the lips of a slanderer and backbiter there is as a fire, not only to brand his neighbor's reputation, to smoke and sully it, but as a burning fire to consume it. And how great a matter does a little of this fire kindle, and how hardly is it extinguished! James 3:5, 6. 2. Such as envy a man the comfort of his friendship, and do all they can to break that, by suggesting that on both sides which will set those at variance that are most nearly related and have been long intimate, or at least cool and alienate their affections one from another: A forward man, that cannot find in his heart to love anybody but himself, is vexed to see others live in love, and therefore makes it is his business to sow strife, by giving men base characters one of another, telling lies, and carrying ill-natured stories between chief friends, so as to separate them one from another, and make them angry at or at least suspicious of one another. Those are bad men and bad women too, that do such ill offices; they are doing the devil's work, and his will their wages be.[135]

16:27. Verses 27-30 refer to troublemakers of various kinds-those who plot evil (v. 27), stir up strife (v. 28), lead others into violence (v. 29), and persist in sin (v. 30). A scoundrel, literally, "a man of belial" (cf. 6:12), is worthless and wicked, and lives in deep moral degradation. He plots evil (cf. 1:10-14; 6:14; 12:20; 14:22; 24:2, 8). "Plots evil" is literally "digs a calamity," which suggests the effort he puts forth to dig a pit to trap others. One of the main ways in which he does this is by words that burn like . . . fire (cf. James 3:5-6).

16:28. A perverse man (lit., "a man of perversity"; see comments on 2:12) stirs up dissension (cf. 6:14, 19; 10:12; 15:18; 28:25; 29:22), causing strife between friends. And by his gossip (cf. 11:13; 18:8; 20:19; 26:20, 22) he causes close friends (cf. 17:9) to doubt and distrust each other.[136]

The worthless man (16:27). "A worthless man (i.e., scoundrel) digs a pit with evil." The reference is to evil words, to slander or words of enticement which are meant to ensnare the innocent. Furthermore, "his speech is like a scorching fire." The words on the lips of the worthless person harm and injure others (cf. James 3:6).

The perverse man (16:28). "A perverse person stirs up strife."

153

The "perverse person" is literally "the person of upside down (utterances)." A person who perverts truth intentionally creates strife and discord. Furthermore, "a backbiter causes a best-friend to separate." Some malicious individuals are determined by their twisted talk to turn one away from his best-friend.[137]

Ver. 27. This and the three following verses are concerned with the case of the evil man. An ungodly man—a man of Belial—diggeth up evil. A man of Belial (ch. 6:12) is a worthless, wicked person, what the French call a vaurien. Such a one digs a pit for others (ch. 26:27; Ps. 7:15), devises mischief against his neighbour, plots against him by lying and slandering and overreaching.

Ver. 28. A froward man soweth strife (ch. 6:14, 19). The verb means, literally, "sends forth," which may signify "scatters as seed" or "hurls as a missile weapon." The character intended is the perverse man, who distorts the truth, gives a wrong impression, attributes evil motives; such a one occasions quarrels and heart burnings. And a whisperer separateth chief friends (ch. 17:9). Nirgan is either "a chatterer," or "a whisperer," "calumniator." In ch. 18:8 and 26:20, 22 it is translated "tale-bearer." "Slanderers," says an old apothegm, "are Satan's bellows to blow up contention." Septuagint, "A perverse man sendeth abroad evils, and kindleth a torch of deceit for the wicked, and separateth friends." 138

13. **Pro. 17:4**

A wicked doer pays attention to false lips;

and a liar pays attention to a naughty tongue.

Commentaries:

Those that design to do ill support themselves by falsehood and lying: A wicked doer gives ear, with a great deal of pleasure, to false lips, that will justify him in the ill he does, to those that aim to make public disturbances, catch greedily at libels, and false stories, that defame the government and the administration. Those that take the liberty to tell lies take a pleasure in hearing them told: A liar gives heed to a malicious backbiting tongue, that he may have something to graft his lies upon, and with which to give them some color of truth and so to support them. Sinners will strengthen one another's hands; and those show that they are bad themselves who court the acquaintance and need the assistance of those that are bad.[139]

Kidner calls this saying "Guilty listener." It is not so much a description of evildoers and liars as a warning against listening to and being influenced by evil words. The same thought is expressed in both lines.

An evildoer listens to wicked lips: An evildoer is a bad or evil person. TEV makes it plural. Listens means pays attention to, follows the advice of. Wicked lips refers to talk such as gossip that aims to cause trouble and to people who spread such talk.

And a liar gives heed to a mischievous tongue: The sense here is that a liar listens to catch anything false so he can pass it on to others. Gives heed has the same sense as listens in line 1. In some languages a liar is called "a person with two tongues" or "a person with a forked tongue." A mischievous tongue is a person who deceives, lies, or says things to create trouble. We may render this line, for example, "Liars listen

to each other" or "Liars pass on
lies they have heard from other
liars." [140]

A wicked person and a liar
both feed on what enhances their
characteristics. They readily
listen to gossip, evil talk that plots
wicked schemes, lies, and
slander. Malicious translates
hawwō, which means "engulfing
ruin, destruction, as
accomplished by one person
against another." (Cf. "gossip" in
11:13; 16:28; 18:8; 20:19; 26:20,
22.) [141]

"An evildoer inclines [the ear]
to wicked lips giving ear to
falsehood upon a destructive
tongue." Such a one listens with
eagerness, and so encourages
the scandal-monger. "Wicked
lips" here point to one who
slanders another. Gossip is
destructive of reputation and
sometimes even of life (17:4). [142]

Taking gossip seriously is
itself a form of malice practiced
by those who have no respect for
the truth. [143]

14. **Pro. 17:9**

The person who that covers a
transgression seeks love;

but the one who repeats accusations separates close friends.

Commentaries:

The way to preserve peace among relations and neighbors is to make the best of everything, not to tell others what has been said or done against them when it is not at all necessary to their safety, nor to take notice of what has been said or done against them when it is not at all necessary to their safety, nor to take notice of what has been said or done against ourselves, but to excuse both, and put the best construction upon them. "It was an oversight; therefore overlook it. It was done through forgetfulness; therefore forget it. It perhaps made nothing of you; do you make nothing of it." 2. The ripping up of faults is the ripping out of love, and nothing tends more to the separating of friends, and setting them at variance, than the repeating of matters that have been in variance; for they commonly lose nothing in the repetition, but the things themselves are aggravated and the passions about them revived and exasperated. The best method of peace is by an amnesty or act of oblivion.[144]

The ability to practice forgiveness and discretion is essential for the survival of an atmosphere of friendship. Probably a whole community and not just a single friendship is in view in v. 9. The covering of an offense would thus include forgiveness but would go beyond it. The "offense" may be against oneself or against a third party. Either way, if a discreet silence is not practiced where appropriate, the atmosphere of trust and mutual love quickly breaks down. The opposite extreme of a forgiving spirit is to take offense and retaliate against those who are only doing good (v. 13). Such a person will not only be friendless but will bring all manner of troubles on his or her head.[145]

He who forgives an offense seeks love: This line should be compared with 10:12, where love is said to "cover all offenses." The motive for forgiveness is love, which refers here to friendly relations with others. As in 10:12, the Hebrew verb used here means "to cover." See there for discussion and for comments on offense. Seeks love means wanting to have good social relations with others. FRCL says "To forgive a wrong fosters friendship," and GECL has "Whoever wishes to keep a friendship forgives offenses." We may also say, for example, "If you wish to have friends, forgive their wrongs."

But he who repeats a matter alienates a friend: This line contrasts with the first. There forgiving wrongs keeps friends, but here talking about a friend's wrongs ruins that friendship. Repeats a matter means "talks repeatedly about a matter," that is, "gossips or tells others about a friend's faults." CEV has "if you keep talking about what they did wrong." Alienates translates a word meaning to separate or divide. To alienate a friend is to make the friend become a stranger or enemy. See 16:28, where RSV translates the same Hebrew expression as "separates close friends." We may translate this whole saying, for example: Whoever forgives a person's wrongs makes friends, but whoever talks about a friend's wrongs loses his friends.[146]

Covering over (see comments on 10:12) an offense is an evidence of love and therefore promotes love. But repeating or gossiping about others' sins can lead friends to be suspicious of each other (cf. 16:28).[147]

He that covers a transgression seeks love; i.e. strives to exercise, put in practice, love (comp. Zeph. 2:3; 1 Cor. 14:4). Thus Nowack. One who bears patiently and silently, extenuates and conceals, something done or said against him, that man follows after charity, obeys the great law of love (comp. ch. 10:12). Some explain the clause to mean, "procures love for himself;" but the second member certainly is not personal, therefore it is more natural to take the first in a general sense. He that repeateth (harpeth on) a matter separates very friends (ch. 16:28). He who is always dwelling on a grievance, returning to it and bringing it forward on every occasion, alienates the greatest friends, only embitters the injury and makes it chronic. Ecclus. 19:7, etc., "Rehearse not unto another that which is told unto thee, and thou shalt fare never the worse. Whether it be to friend or foe, talk not of other men's lives; and if thou canst without offence, reveal them not. For he heard and observed thee, and when time cometh he will hate thee. If thou hast heard a word, let it die with thee; and be bold, it will not burst thee." So the rabbis said: "Abstain from quarrels with thy neighbor; and if thou hast seen something bad of thy friend, let it not pass thy tongue as a slander" (Dukes, § 61). The Mosaic Law had led the way to this duty of forbearance: "Thou shalt not avenge, nor bear any grudge against the children of thy people, but thou shalt love thy neighbor as thyself" (Lev. 19:18). Septuagint, "He who concealeth injuries seeketh friendship; but he who hateth to conceal them separateth friends and households." [148]

15. **Pro. 18:8**

The words of a gossiper are like tasty morsels,

and they go down into the innermost parts of the belly.

Commentaries:

"The words of a whisperer are like choice morsels, and they go down to the depths of the belly." A "whisperer" (nirgan) is a gossip. The juicy tidbits of gossip are eagerly devoured by persons disposed to listen to them, as a glutton helps himself freely to tempting food. The slanderous words do not make a superficial impression, but penetrate into the innermost recesses of the listener where they are thoroughly digested. They are treasured up in memory to be used as occasion may offer. [149]

"A whisperer's words are received with avidity; calumny, slander, and evil stories find eager listeners." The same metaphor is found in ch. 19:28; Job 34:7. There may, at the same time, be involved the idea that these dainty morsels are of poisonous character. Vulgate, Verba bilinguis, quasi simplicia, "The words of a man of double tongue seem to be simple," which contains another truth. They go down into the innermost parts of the belly (ch. 20:27, 30). The hearers take in the slanders and treasure them up in memory, to be used as occasion shall offer." [150]

Gossip (cf. 11:13; 16:28; 26:20) is like choice morsels (lit., "things greedily devoured," a Hebrew word used only here and in 26:22, which is identical with 18:8). Hearing gossip is like eating a delicacy (something not everyone else hears). Therefore, like food being digested,

163

gossiped news is assimilated in one's innermost parts (i.e, is retained and remembered). [151]

Tale-bearers are those who secretly carry stories from house to house, which perhaps have some truth in them, but are secrets not fit to be told, or are basely misrepresented, and false colors put upon them, and are all told with design to blast men's reputation, to break their friendship, to make mischief between relations and neighbors, and set them at variance. [152]

16. **Pro. 18:13**

He that makes up his mind before hearing the entire issue, will bring folly and shame to himself.

Commentaries:

See here how men often expose themselves by that very thing by which they hope to gain applause. 1. Some take a pride in being quick. They answer a matter before they hear it, hear it out, nay, as soon as they but hear of it. They think it is their honor to take up a cause suddenly; and, when they have heard one side, they think the matter so plain that they need not trouble themselves to hear the other; they are already apprised of it, and masters of all the merits of the cause. Whereas, though a ready wit is an agreeable thing to play with, it is solid judgment and sound wisdom that do business. 2. Those that take a pride in being quick commonly fall under the just reproach of being impertinent. It is folly for a man to go about to speak to a thing which he does not understand, or to pass sentence upon a matter which he is not truly and fully informed of, and has not patience to make a strict enquiry into; and, if it be folly, it is and will be shame. [153]

17. **Pro. 18:17**

The first person who presents his side may seem to be just; but his neighbor (i.e. the defendant) will come and interrogate him.

Commentaries:

This shows that one tale is good till another is told. 1. He that speaks first will be sure to tell a straight story, and relate that only which makes for him, and put the best color he can upon it, so that his cause shall appear good, whether it really be so or no. 2. The plaintiff having done his evidence, it is fit that the defendant should be heard, should have leave to confront the witnesses and cross-examine them, and show the falsehood and fallacy of what has been alleged, which perhaps may make the matter appear quite otherwise than it did. We must therefore remember that we have two ears, to hear both sides before we give judgment. [154]

"The first in presenting his case seems right; his neighbor comes and searches him out." The plaintiff who states his case first puts forward the evidence which puts him in the best possible light. When he is finished, it looks as though he must be in the right. His neighbor—the defendant—comes and searches out the other's case, i.e., he brings evidence forward which places the previous testimony in question. Thus judges must not come to a conclusion until both sides are heard. [155]

18. **Pro. 20:19**

The person who runs around spreading gossip reveals "secret" information, but do not have anything to do with him as he flatters you with his lips.

Commentaries:

Two sorts of people are dangerous to be conversed with: 1. Tale-bearers, though they are commonly flatterers, and by fair speeches insinuate themselves into men's acquaintance. Those are unprincipled people that go about carrying stories, that make mischief among neighbours and relations, that sow in the minds of people jealousies of their governors, of their ministers, and of one another, that reveal secrets which they are entrusted with or which by unfair means they come to the knowledge of, under pretence of guessing at men's thoughts and intentions, tell that of them which is really false. "Be not familiar with such; do not give them the hearing when they tell their tales and reveal secrets, for you may be sure that they will betray your secrets too and tell tales of you."

2. Flatterers, for they are commonly tale-bearers. If a man fawn upon you, compliment and commend you, suspect him to have some design upon you, and stand upon your guard; he would pick that out of you which will serve him to make a story of to somebody else to your prejudice; therefore meddle not with him that flatters with his lips. Those too dearly love, and too dearly buy, their own praise, that will put confidence in a man and trust

him with a secret or business because he flatters them.[156]

"One who reveals secrets is one who goes about as a talebearer; so do not mix with one who opens wide his lips" (cf.11:13). One should not associate with a gossiper who spreads confidential information. He cannot be trusted with any secret; therefore one must exercise caution in what is said to him. One who "opens wide his lips" is one who cannot keep his mouth shut. [157]

19. **Pro. 24:28-29**

Do not accuse your neighbor without just cause and do not lie with your lips.

Say not,

"I will do so to him as he hath done to me:

I will render to the man according to his work."

Commentaries:

Giving false testimony-and thereby harming some-one's reputation or unjustly acquiring things from him, or even taking his life-is frequently forbidden in Proverbs (see comments on 6:19). It is prohibited by the ninth commandment (Ex. 20:16). Being deceptive in what one says in court is wrong-(see comments on "deceit" in Prov. 12:20).[158]

We are here forbidden to be in anything injurious to our neighbor, particularly in and by the forms of law, either, 1. As a witness: "Never bear a testimony against any man without cause, unless what thou sayest thou knowest to be punctually true and thou hast a clear call to testify it. Never bear a false testimony against any one;" for it follows, "Deceive not with thy lips; deceive not the judge and jury, deceive not those whom thou converses with, into an ill opinion of thy neighbor. When thou speak of thy neighbor do not only speak that which is true, but take heed lest, in the manner of thy speaking, thou insinuate anything that is otherwise and so should deceive by innuendos or hyperboles." Or, 2. As a plaintiff or prosecutor. If there be occasion to bring an action or information against thy neighbor, let it not be from a spirit of revenge. "Say not, I am resolved I will be even with him: I will do so to him as he had done to me." Even a righteous cause becomes unrighteous when it is thus prosecuted with malice. Say not, I will render to the man according to his work, and make him pay dearly for it; for it is God's prerogative to do so, and we must leave it to him, and not step into his throne, or take his work out of his hands. If we will needs be our own carvers, and judges in our own cause, we forfeit the benefit of an appeal to God's tribunal; therefore we must not avenge ourselves, because he has said, Vengeance is mine. [159]

20. **Pro. 25:8-10**

Do not rush out in public to argue your case because,

in the end, what will you do when your neighbor puts you to shame publicly?

Instead, argue your case with your neighbor in private,

and do not reveal confidential matters to others

lest those who hear you will publicly rebuke you,

and an evil report about you will not soon pass away.

Commentaries:

The rabbis understood verse 9 as calling for discussion of the matter with one's neighbor. If the matter is settled in your favor, you're not to "betray a confidence" and tell everyone what your neighbor did wrong.

Verse 10 shows that anyone who betrays confidences soon loses the trust of others to work out fair and private resolutions in the future. [160]

First, do not rush into public conflict, certain that right is on your side, nor if you make it a private matter, reveal all your sources; either way you may end up humiliated (8–10). Don't lose your self-control, or you may find you have lost everything (28). [161]

Ver. 9—Debate thy cause with thy neighbor himself (Matt. 18:15; see on ver. 8). If you have any quarrel with a neighbor, or are drawn into a controversy with him, deal with him privately in a friendly manner. And discover not a secret to another; rather, the secret of another. Do not bring in a third party, or make use of anything entrusted to you by another person, or of which you have become privately informed, in order to support your cause. [162]

Our first desire is to "tell the whole world" and get everybody on our side. But the Bible counsels just the opposite: talk to the person alone and do not allow others to interfere. This is what Jesus commanded in Matt. 18:15–17, and if this policy were followed in families and churches, there would be fewer fights and splits. It is sad when professing Christians tell everybody but the one involved. Certainly, it takes courage and Christian love to talk over a difference with a brother or sister, but this is the way to grow spiritually and to glorify Christ.[163]

Perhaps the matter in variance is a secret, not fit to be divulged to any, much less to be brought upon the stage before the country; and therefore end it privately, that it may not be discovered." Reveal not the secret of another, so some read it. "Do not, in revenge, to disgrace thy adversary, disclose that which should be kept private and which does not at all belong to the cause."[164]

Argue your case with your neighbor himself: Argue your case in this context means to discuss differences of opinion, and with your neighbor himself means "privately." And do not disclose another's secret: Disclose renders a word meaning "uncover" and refers to making something public, exposing it to the public, or telling others about it. A secret refers to information that one of the parties to the dispute has learned about the

172

other. REB translates "Argue your own case with your neighbor, and do not reveal another's secrets." In some languages we may also say, for example, "Exchange words with your friend, but do not tell others what you have learned about him." A translation in a Pacific language says: "If you and your neighbor have a row about something, it is best for just you-two to sort it out, and afterwards you must not talk about this private business."[165]

A courtier should not betray confidences. In an argument with a neighbor the temptation exists to reveal secret information about him. A person who betrays confidential information will be reviled as a talebearer by those who hear him. His bad reputation would remain with him forever (25:9–10).[166]

Debate thy cause with thy neighbor himself (Matt. 18:15; see on ver. 8). If you have any quarrel with a neighbor, or are drawn into a controversy with him, deal with him privately in a friendly manner. And discover not a secret to another; rather, the secret of another. Do not bring in a third party, or make use of anything entrusted to you by another person, or of which you have become privately informed, in order to support your cause.

Ver. 10.—Lest he that heareth it put thee to shame; i. e. lest anyone, not the offended neighbor only, who hears how treacherous you have been, makes your proceeding known and cries shame upon you. [167]

Dissension under any circumstances is a serious evil. The considerate Christian will rather conceded rights, than insist upon them to the hazard of his own soul, and to the injury of the Church. (1 Cor. v.1-7). Hasty strife must always be wrong. Think well beforehand, whether the case be right, or even if it be, whether it worth the contention. Duly calculate the uncertainty or consequence of the end.

So long as "meum and tuum" are in the world, sin and Satan will stir up contention. Yet never forget, that not "hatred and wrath" only, but "variance and strife" are "works of the flesh," excluding from heaven (Gal. v. 19-21). Hence the constraining obligation to "seek peace, and pursue it" (Ps. Xxxiv. 14); after the noble example of our father Abraham, who quenched "the

174

beginning of the strife," by yielding to his nephew his natural superiority, and his just rights. (Gen. xiii. 8 Comp. chap. Xvii. 14.)...How many unholy heats would be restrained by the practice of these rules of wisdom and love! [168]

21. **Pro. 26:17**

Like someone who seizes the ears of a passing dog is the person who interjects himself in issues that

do not involve him personally.

Commentaries:

That which is here condemned is meddling with strife that belongs not to us. If we must not be hasty to strive in our own cause (ch. 25:8), much less in other people's, especially theirs that we are no way related to or concerned in, but light on accidentally as we pass by. If we can be instrumental to make peace between those that are at variance we must do it, though we should thereby get the ill-will of both sides, at least while they are in their heat; but to make ourselves busy in other men's matters, and parties in other men's quarrels, is not only to court our own trouble, but to thrust ourselves into temptation.

Who made me a judge? Let them end it, as they began it, between themselves. 2. We are cautioned against it because of the danger it exposes us to; it is like taking a snarling dog by the ears, that will snap at you and bite you; you had better have let him alone, for you cannot get clear of him when you would, and must thank yourselves if you come off with a wound and dishonor. He that has got a dog by the ears, if he lets him go he flies at him, if he keeps his hold, he has his hands full, and can do nothing else. Let everyone with quietness work and mind his own business, and not with unquietness quarrel and meddle with other people's business. [169]

Verses 17-28 refer to quarrels (vv. 17, 20-21), deceit (vv. 18-19, 24-26), gossip (vv. 20, 22), and lying (vv. 23, 28). One who grabs a dog by its ears may expect to be bitten. So is a passer-by, someone not directly involved, who meddles in (lit., "excites himself over") another's quarrel. He causes trouble for himself by interfering in a situation he knows little about. [170]

Busybodies cannot resist the temptation to inject themselves into private disputes, and they have no excuse for being surprised at the violent outbursts that are sure to follow. [171]

Note: The longer I live, the more I realize that most issues are none of my business and I should refrain from getting involved in things that do not directly pertain to me, my family, church or nation.

22. **Pro. 26:28**

A lying tongue hates those who are afflicted by it;

and a flattering mouth works ruin.

Commentaries:

The next series of proverbs deals with malicious, especially deceitful, persons who disseminate their hatred under a cloak of friendship. Gossips love to hear gossip. The words of a whisperer are as "dainty morsels," i.e., something delightful. They are taken into the innermost parts of the body, i.e., they are eaten and digested (26:22; cf. 18:8).

Hypocrites express friendship fervently with their lips. Yet the hearts of such people are wicked. They plot the ruin of the others who are lulled into a false sense of security by their "burning [fervent] lips." Such people are like "the silver of

177

dross," i.e., the base metal which is left when the pure silver has been refined. This inferior silver was used to overlay earthenware and gave the vessel the appearance of being valuable. The point is that a glittering exterior often hides the reality within (26:23).

Some people are full of hatred, yet they feign friendship by friendly speech. Such a person "lays up" deceit until an opportunity occurs to vent the animosity. The teacher advises his readers to put no trust in the pleasant words of such a man. Within the heart of that man are "seven abominations," i.e., countless wicked-ness. Hatred is frequently concealed with deceit. Sooner or later that hatred finds expression in some vicious act. The matter is then brought before the public assembly acting in a judicial capacity. At that time the fate of the hater is made clear (26:24–26).

The person who maliciously digs a pit with the intention of injuring another, shall fall therein. Whoever attempts to roll a stone upon another shall be crushed by that same stone. This refers to rolling stones up to a height in order to hurl them down upon an enemy (26:27).

A liar selects as the objects of his slander those whom he hates. The person with a "smooth mouth" conceals his real thoughts. His intention is to bring about somebody's downfall (26:28). [172]

People who lie are actually hateful (see comments on malice in v. 26); they desire to harm others by slandering their reputations. And people who flatter to help achieve their selfishly deceptive ends (cf. vv. 23-26) bring ruin either to themselves, their victims, or both. [173]

23. **Pro. 29:9**

When a wise man attempts to refute a fool,

The fool either rages or laughs at him, and there will be no peaceful conclusion.

Commentaries:

A wise man is here advised not to set his wit to a fool's, not to dispute with him, or by contending with him to think either of fastening reason upon him or gaining right from him: If a wise man contend with a wise man, he may hope to be understood, and, as far as he has reason and equity on his side, to carry his point, at least to bring the controversy to a head and make it issue amicably; but, if he contend with a foolish man, there is no rest; he will see no end of it, nor will he have any satisfaction in it, but must expect to be always uneasy. 1. Whether the foolish man he contends with rage or laugh, whether he take angrily or scornfully what is said to him, whether he rail at it or mock at it, one of the two he will do, and so there will be no rest. However it is given, it will be ill-taken, and the wisest man must expect to be either scolded or ridiculed if he contend with a fool. He that fights with a dunghill, whether he be conqueror or conquered, is sure to be defiled. 2. Whether the wise man himself rage or laugh, whether he take the serious or the jocular way of dealing with the fool, whether he be severe or pleasant with him, whether he come with a rod or with the spirit of meekness (1 Co. 4:21), it is all alike, no good is done. We have piped unto you, and you have not danced, mourned unto you, and you have not lamented. [174]

If a wise man has an argument with a fool...The fool

only rages and laughs, and there is no quiet... there is no quiet may refer to the impossibility of resolving the dispute with the fool. In this case we may say, for example, "and there is no satisfaction" or "and there is no quiet solution."... for example, "he will only speak with anger and abuse, and will not shut his mouth." [175]

To try to argue with a fool is futile. He will either laugh off the arguments, or he will get angry. In either case the discussion leads nowhere. The issue will not be resolved (29:9). [176]

...after all has been said, the fool only falls into a passion or laughs at the matter, argument is wasted upon him, and the controversy is never settled. [177]

24. **Pro. 30:10**

Do not slander a slave to his master,

Lest he curse you and you are found guilty.

Commentaries:

One should be hesitant to impugn a laborer to his master (or, in modern terms, to his employer). Otherwise one will be subject to verbal retaliation and be guilty of being a meddler. Behind this injunction is a demand that one respect the person of the menial worker. His work relationship with his master is between the two of them; one should no more interfere here than one would interfere in a matter involving a superior or an equal.[178]

This verse is a warning not to meddle in another person's domestic affairs. A master may curse the person who falsely accuses his servant. In contrast with the "undeserved curse" of 26:2, this curse will "hit its target" so to speak, because it is deserved.[179]

Three units relate to each other here. Cursing is the verbal link between the saying in v 10 and the longer unit vs 11–14. The former warns against interfering in other people's affairs in a way that may rebound; he might be master or servant.[180]

This verse is a short saying that warns against criticizing a servant to his master. Do not slander a servant to his master: The verb slander is related to the word "tongue" and has the sense of "gossip about" or "say bad things about" a person.   Scott   gives   the   title "Talebearing" to this saying.[181]

Note: Pastors should refrain from interfering with the hiring or firing of employees of other churches. Such internal business issues are none of their business.

Conclusion

We have examined the biblical condemnation of slander and gossip from Genesis to Revelation. It is documented and condemned more than any other sin mentioned in the Bible. Yet, many professing Christians today are creating, receiving, and passing on gossip and slander of the grossest kinds against dear pastors, missionaries, elders, deacons, and Christian leaders. Men and women who have sacrificed everything to preach the gospel to the lost and to comfort the saved are maligned and ridiculed in the most unkind ways.

What shall we then say about the present orgy of slander and gossip that fills the internet? It is a wicked and vile abomination condemned by God as a sin that is not compatible with a Christian profession of faith. Those who live in the sins of slander and gossip must be judged as unregenerate and degenerate until they repent at the foot of the cross.

Job's "friends" had slandered and gossiped against him in many ways and said things against him that were not true. When God spoke from the wind, He demanded that they go to Job in abject humility, ask his forgiveness, and plead that he would pray for them and offer a sacrifice that would avert the judgment of God upon them. In the same way, those who today have a "ministry" of slander and gossip must go to those they slandered and ask for their forgiveness and prayers. If they do not repent of their slander and gossip, they forever demonstrate that they are the children of the devil.

The wisest man who ever lived, King Solomon, told us how to deal with slanderers, gossipers, mockers, talebearers, and scoffers in Pro. 22:10.

Drive out the scoffer and contention will go out,

Even strife and dishonor will cease.

The Apostle likewise commanded in Rom. 16:17-18 and Tit. 3:10 that churches should cast out all slanderers, gossip mongers, mockers, scoffers, and schismatics as apostates. They should be denied Holy Communion and placed under church discipline.

Commentaries:

A mocker (cf. 9:7-8, 12; 13:1; 14:6; 15:12; 19:25, 29; 21:11, 24; 24:9) causes strife (contention), quarreling, and insults (qālôn, "disgrace"; used eight times in Prov. and only nine times elsewhere). So by removing a troublemaker, trouble also leaves.

1. What the scorner does. It is implied that he sows discord and makes mischief wherever he comes. Much of the strife and contention which disturb the peace of all societies is owing to the evil interpreter (as some read it), that construes everything into the worst, to those that despise and deride every one that comes in their way and take a pride in bantering and abusing all mankind. 2. What is to be done with the scorner that will not be reclaimed: Cast him out of your

186

society, as Ishmael, when he mocked Isaac, was thrust out of Abraham's family. Those that would secure the peace must exclude the scorner.[182]

This verse is an observation about human behavior: a person with the wrong attitude can be the cause of much trouble and strife, which will cease if the troublemaker is removed from the situation. The second line adds a clause that parallels and extends the meaning of the last part of the first line. Drive out a scoffer, and strife will go out: For a scoffer see the comments at 1:22. In this context the focus is probably on the person's attitude of conceit and disrespect for others, expressed in speech that insults or hurts. TEV "a conceited person" and CEV "those who insult others" express this well. Drive out may also be expressed in English by such words as "expel" (NJB, Scott), "banish" (REB), and "get rid of" (TEV). For the term translated strife see 10:12; see also 6:14, 19 (RSV "discord") and 18:19; 26:20 (RSV "quarreling"). Will go out means that the trouble will go away or disappear, it "will come to an end" (CEV), "there will be no more arguments" (TEV). In a number of languages the natural way to express this is "[fighting talk] will finish." And quarreling and abuse will cease: The Septuagint reflects a different text for this line; but hardly any modern versions follow it, and HOTTP recommends following the Hebrew ("B" rating). The whole line is parallel and similar in meaning to strife will go out in the first line. The term translated quarreling mostly has the sense of "judgment" or "condemnation" and hence "legal strife" or "lawsuits" (NJB); in this context, however, it seems to have a more general sense of "quarreling" or "argument." Abuse means basically "disgrace" or "dishonor," and in particular the sort of talk that inflicts dishonor or shame on others. It is well translated as "insults" (NIV) or "name-calling" (Scott, TEV). Will cease means "will end," "will come to an end" (CEV), or "will disappear." Since the terms of the second line are very similar in meaning to strife in the first line, it is possible to restructure the verse to bring these terms together; for example, "Arguments and fights will come to an end, if you chase away those who insult others" (CEV). See TEV also. [183]

In v. 10 the speaker is an obnoxious (and possibly litigious) troublemaker. One can restore harmony to a situation by removing such people. By contrast, those whose minds and words are peaceable find themselves welcomed on the highest level (v. 11) rather than being driven away. [184]

Cast out the scorner, and contention shall go out; Septuagint, ἔκβαλε ἐκ συνεδρίου λοιμόν, "Cast out of the company a pestilent fellow." Chase away the scorner (ch. 1:22), the man who has no respect for things human or Divine, and the disputes and ill feeling which he caused will be ended; for "where no wood is, the fire goeth out" (ch. 26:20). Yea, strife and reproach shall cease. The reproach and ignominy (קָלוֹן kalon) are those which the presence and words of the scorner bring with them; to have such a one in the company is a disgrace to all good men. Thus Ishmael and his mother were driven from Abraham's dwelling (Gen. 21:9, etc.), and the apostle quotes (Gal. 4:30), "Cast out (ἔκβαλε) the bondwoman and her son." Septuagint, "For when he sits in the company he dishonors all." [185]

I close with an illustration from my old friend, Dr. Jay Adams. In his landmark book, *The Christian Counselor's Manual*, he relates the following counseling case:

> At a pastor's conference the following case was mentioned:

> Pastor: "A husband and wife were spreading gossip about the church board throughout our congregation and to other nearby congregations. Here is what we did: an elder and the pastor visited them during the regular yearly house visitation program. The couple brought up their problem with the board. A long discussion followed. The pastor and elder tried to clear up any misunderstanding of the board's position. This began and ended with the reading of the Scriptures and with prayer. We said that if we had hurt or offended them in any way, we were sorry. The husband and wife are continuing to gossip about the church board and are very critical about everything. What should we have done? What can we do now?"

> It seems there were several things that should have been done differently. For example, the visit was made during regular yearly house visitation; that is to say, a special

visit was not made. If there was gossip going on, a special visit should have been made to deal specifically with that problem. The problem already was on a level that involved the church. It was not the private level or the one-or-two others level. The gossipers had put the matter in to the public domain. The gossip had spread through the congregation and to other congregations and pastors. The problem already had reached the highest level. Therefore, the pastor and elders were correct in considering the matter as a board.

But the manner of the visit that was conducted obscured the visitors' purpose. The people involved in the alleged sin were given no reason to believe that they were being visited to be dealt with about their gossip; there is no indication that they were. As a matter of fact, the problem with the board was raised not by the visitors, but by the sinning couple themselves. Yet, even then, the pastor and elder continued to speak not about the gossip, but rather whether the board was right or wrong. They succumbed to the temptation to take an "easier" way out...Instead of these mild,

191

oblique approaches, we must learn, in such cases, to be ironically direct...Instead, the visitors should have focused their comments directly upon the question of gossip. The issue concerning the board should have been separated from the issue of gossip...The allegedly gossiping members were not prepared to pluck a splinter from the board's eye until the plank in their own eye was removed.

The pastor and the elder were on the defensive rather than the offensive. They were failing to exercise the authority of Christ vested in them...the main point is that nothing was said about the gossip.

Gossip is a very destructive sin; for the glory of God, the welfare of His church, and the sake of the offenders, it should have been dealt with. No wonder these members are continuing to gossip; nobody ever talked to them about that. No wonder they are very critical about everything.[186]

Dr. Adams points out the main failure of so many pastors today. They are so afraid of losing church members (and their offerings) that they do not rebuke gossipers "with all authority" as Scripture commands (Tit. 2:15). If those rebuked reject pastoral admonition, they should be "delivered over to Satan" in obedience to the Word of God (1

Cor. 5:1-5 cf. 1 Tim. 1:19-20). In other words, too many pastors are cowards and do not have the guts to rebuke, admonish, and condemn sin in their own church. They want everyone to like them!

Things get even more complicated when you rebuke and put under church discipline gossip-mongers and they run off to another church where the pastor gives them a sympathetic ear. He allows them to slander their previous church, its board, and pastor without rebuking them. He does not care if they set up slander sites on the internet where they attack their previous church with malicious hatred and spite. In order to please the gossipers, he joins them in spreading their gossip and slander. Some wicked pastors have even mounted their own slander campaign to destroy other churches and pastors! These busybodies cause great damage to the reputation of Jesus in the community by falling into the sins of slander and gossip.

Pastors, missionaries, and Christian leaders must understand that if they choose to obey Scripture when dealing with gossipers and slanderers, they will be condemned more viciously than the gossipers. Placing gossipers under church discipline is viewed today as being *more evil* than the sin of gossip! But, those who live for the smile of God care not for the frown of man. They will apply the Lordship of Christ to all of life including slander and gossip. They will not be intimidated by cowardly pastors who engage in slander and gossip.

Dear man or woman of God, do not retreat, give in, give up, give way, be bought off or frightened off by the wrath of man. Be bold in your God. Obey Scripture and if the world, churches or ministerial associations condemn you for doing so, take to heart Paul's admonition in 1 Cor. 15:59.

Therefore, my beloved brethren, be steadfast, immovable, always abounding in the work of the Lord, knowing that your toil is not *in* vain in the Lord.

Amen and Amen!

Endnotes

1. Hammond, Peter and Abshire, Brian, *Character Assassins: Dealing with Ecclesiastical Tyrants and Terrorists*, (Cape Town: Christian Liberty Books, 2004).

2. Rediger, Lloyd, *Clergy Killers: Guidance for Pastors and Congregations Under Attack*, (MN: Logos, 1997)

3. Greenfield, Guy, *The Wounded Minister: Healing from and Preventing Personal Attacks*, (Grand Rapids: Baker, 2001)

4. www.faithdefenders.com

5. Henry, Matthew: Matthew Henry's Commentary on the Whole Bible : Complete and Unabridged in One Volume. Peabody : Hendrickson, 1996, c1991, S. Lk 6:20

6. Morey, Robert, The Bible, Natural Law, and Natural Theology: Conflict or Compromise?, (P.O. Box 240, Millerstown, PA 17062, 2009)

7. Walvoord, John F. ; Zuck, Roy B. ; Dallas Theological Seminary: The Bible Knowledge Commentary : An Exposition of the Scriptures. Wheaton, IL : Victor Books, 1983-c1985, S. 1:719-720

8. Henry, Matthew: Matthew Henry's Commentary on the Whole Bible: Complete and Unabridged in One Volume. Peabody : Hendrickson, 1996, c1991, S. Job 1:6

9. Smith, James E.: The Wisdom Literature and Psalms. Joplin, Mo. : College Press Pub. Co., 1996, S. Job 1:6-12

10. Spence-Jones, H. D. M. (Hrsg.): The Pulpit Commentary: Job. Bellingham, WA : Logos Research Systems, Inc., 2004, S. 4

11. Walvoord, John F. ; Zuck, Roy B. ; Dallas Theological Seminary: The Bible Knowledge Commentary : An Exposition of the Scriptures. Wheaton, IL : Victor Books, 1983-c1985, S. 1:721

12. Henry, Matthew: Matthew Henry's Commentary on the Whole Bible: Complete and Unabridged in One Volume. Peabody : Hendrickson, 1996, c1991, S. Job 2:1

13. Walvoord, John F. ; Zuck, Roy B. ; Dallas Theological Seminary: The Bible Knowledge Commentary : An Exposition of the Scriptures. Wheaton, IL : Victor Books, 1983-c1985, S. 1:719-720

14. Willmington, H. L.: The Outline Bible. Wheaton, Ill. : Tyndale House Publishers, 1999, S. Nu 16:1-50

15. Smith, James E.: The Pentateuch. 2nd ed. Joplin, Mo. : College Press Pub. Co., 1993, S. Nu 16:1-50

16. Wiersbe, Warren W.: Wiersbe's Expository Outlines on the Old Testament. Wheaton, IL : Victor Books, 1993, S. Nu 16:1

17. Carson, D. A.: New Bible Commentary : 21st Century Edition. 4th ed. Leicester, England; Downers Grove, Ill., USA : Inter-Varsity Press, 1994, S. Nu 16:1-16

18. Walvoord, John F. ; Zuck, Roy B. ; Dallas Theological Seminary: The Bible Knowledge Commentary : An Exposition of the Scriptures. Wheaton, IL : Victor Books, 1983-c1985, S. 1:233-234

19. Jamieson, Robert ; Fausset, A. R. ; Fausset, A. R. ; Brown, David ; Brown, David: A Commentary, Critical and Explanatory, on the Old and New Testaments. Oak Harbor, WA : Logos Research Systems, Inc., 1997, S. Nu 16:4

20. Lange, John Peter ; Schaff, Philip ; Lowrie, Samuel T. ; Gosman, A.: A Commentary on the Holy Scriptures : Numbers. Bellingham, WA : Logos Research Systems, Inc., 2008, S. 8

21. Cole, R. Dennis: Numbers. electronic ed. Nashville : Broadman & Holman Publishers, 2001, c2000 (Logos Library System; The New American Commentary 3B), S. 261

22. Cole, R. Dennis: Numbers. electronic ed. Nashville : Broadman & Holman Publishers, 2001, c2000 (Logos Library System; The New American Commentary 3B), S. 263

23. Walvoord, John F. ; Zuck, Roy B. ; Dallas Theological Seminary: The Bible knowledge commentary : an exposition of the scriptures. Wheaton, IL : Victor Books, 1983-c1985, S. 1:677

24. Wiersbe, Warren W.: Be Determined. Wheaton, Ill. : Victor Books, 1996, c1992, S. Ne 2:11

25. Walvoord, John F. ; Zuck, Roy B. ; Dallas Theological Seminary: The Bible Knowledge Commentary : An Exposition of the Scriptures. Wheaton, IL : Victor Books, 1983-c1985, S. 1:681

26. Carson, D. A.: New Bible Commentary : 21st Century Edition. 4th ed. Leicester, England; Downers Grove, Ill., USA : Inter-Varsity Press, 1994, S. Ne 4:1

27. Wiersbe, Warren W.: Be Determined. Wheaton, Ill. : Victor Books, 1996, c1992, S. Ne 4:1

28. Wiersbe, Warren W.: Wiersbe's Expository Outlines on the Old

Testament. Wheaton, IL : Victor Books, 1993, S. Ne 4:1

29.   Wiersbe, Warren W.: Be Determined. Wheaton, Ill. : Victor Books, 1996, c1992, S. Ne 4:7

30.   Wiersbe, Warren W.: Be Determined. Wheaton, Ill. : Victor Books, 1996, c1992, S. Ne 4:10

31.   Wiersbe, Warren W.: Be Determined. Wheaton, Ill. : Victor Books, 1996, c1992, S. Ne 4:11

32.   Walvoord, John F. ; Zuck, Roy B. ; Dallas Theological Seminary: The Bible Knowledge Commentary : An Exposition of the Scriptures. Wheaton, IL : Victor Books, 1983-c1985, S. 1:682

33.   Walvoord, John F. ; Zuck, Roy B. ; Dallas Theological Seminary: The Bible Knowledge Commentary : An Exposition of the Scriptures. Wheaton, IL : Victor Books, 1983-c1985, S. 1:682

34.   For a full discussion of the devil schemes, see: Robert Morey, Satan's Devices, (PO Box 240, Millerstown, PA, 17062: Christian Scholars Press, 2006).

35.   Henry, Matthew: Matthew Henry's Commentary on the Whole Bible : Complete and Unabridged in One Volume. Peabody : Hendrickson, 1996, c1991, S. Mt 11:16

36. Hendriksen, William ; Kistemaker, Simon J.: New Testament Commentary : Exposition of the Gospel According to Matthew. Grand Rapids : Baker Book House, 1953-2001 (New Testament Commentary 9), S. 492

37. Walvoord, John F. ; Zuck, Roy B. ; Dallas Theological Seminary: The Bible Knowledge Commentary : An Exposition of the Scriptures. Wheaton, IL : Victor Books, 1983-c1985, S. 2:117-118

38. Carson, D. A.: New Bible Commentary : 21st Century Edition. 4th ed. Leicester, England; Downers Grove, Ill., USA : Inter-Varsity Press, 1994, S. Mk 3:20

39. Hendriksen, William ; Kistemaker, Simon J.: New Testament Commentary : Exposition of the Gospel According to Mark. Grand Rapids : Baker Book House, 1953-2001 (New Testament Commentary 10), S. 135

40. Henry, Matthew: Matthew Henry's Commentary on the Whole Bible : Complete and Unabridged in One Volume. Peabody : Hendrickson, 1996, c1991, S. Mt 28:11

41. Carson, D. A.: New Bible Commentary : 21st Century Edition. 4th ed. Leicester, England; Downers Grove, Ill., USA : Inter-Varsity Press, 1994, S. Mt 28:1

42. Walvoord, John F. ; Zuck, Roy B. ; Dallas Theological Seminary: The Bible Knowledge Commentary : An Exposition

of the Scriptures. Wheaton, IL : Victor Books, 1983-c1985, S. 1:298

43. Jamieson, Robert ; Fausset, A. R. ; Fausset, A. R. ; Brown, David ; Brown, David: A Commentary, Critical and Explanatory, on the Old and New Testaments. Oak Harbor, WA : Logos Research Systems, Inc., 1997, S. Dt 19:15

44. Henry, Matthew: Matthew Henry's Commentary on the Whole Bible : Complete and Unabridged in One Volume. Peabody : Hendrickson, 1996, c1991, S. Dt 19:14

45. Keil, Carl Friedrich ; Delitzsch, Franz: Commentary on the Old Testament. Peabody, MA : Hendrickson, 2002, S. 1:938

46. Calvin, John, Commentaries on the Last Four Books of Moses, (Grand Rapids: Eerdmans, n.d.), III:45

47. Cummings, John, Deuteronomy, (Minneapolis: Klock & Klock, 1982), p. 259.

48. Henry, Matthew: Matthew Henry's Commentary on the Whole Bible: Complete and Unabridged in One Volume. Peabody : Hendrickson, 1996, c1991, S. Ps 16:1

49. Lange, John Peter; Schaff, Philip; Moll, Carl Bernhard; Briggs, Charles A.; Forsyth, D. D.; Hammond, James B ;

McCurdy, J. Frederick; Conant, Thomas
J.: A Commentary on the Holy Scripture :
Psalms. Bellingham, WA: Logos
Research Systems, Inc., 2008, S. 118

50. Walvoord, John F.; Zuck, Roy B.; Dallas
Theological Seminary: The Bible
Knowledge Commentary: An Exposition
of the Scriptures. Wheaton, IL : Victor
Books, 1983-c1985, S. 1:803

51. Jamieson, Robert ; Fausset, A. R. ;
Fausset, A. R. ; Brown, David ; Brown,
David: A Commentary, Critical and
Explanatory, on the Old and New
Testaments. Oak Harbor, WA : Logos
Research Systems, Inc., 1997, S. Ps 15:1

52. Carson, D. A.: New Bible Commentary:
21st Century Edition. 4th ed. Leicester,
England; Downers Grove, Ill., USA : Inter-
Varsity Press, 1994, S. Ps 15:1

53. Bratcher, Robert G. ; Reyburn, William
David: A Translator's Handbook on the
Book of Psalms. New York : United Bible
Societies, 1991 (Helps for Translators), S.
136

54. Spence-Jones, H. D. M. (Hrsg.): The
Pulpit Commentary: Psalms Vol. I.
Bellingham, WA : Logos Research
Systems, Inc., 2004, S. 91

55. Richards, Lawrence O.: The Bible
Readers Companion. electronic ed.
Wheaton : Victor Books, 1991; Published
in electronic form by Logos Research
Systems, 1996, S. 353

56. H. C. Leupold, Exposition of Psalms, (Grand Rapids: Baker, 1961), p. 145.

57. William Plumer, Psalms, (Edinburgh: Banner of Truth, 1975), p. 201.

58. J. A. Alexander, The Psalms, (Grand Rapids: Zondervan, n.d.), p. 64.

59. John Calvin, Psalms, (Grand Rapids: Eerdmans, 1963), I:206-207.

60. Charles Spurgeon, Treasury of David, (Grand Rapids: Zondervan, 1969), I:184-185, 191.

61. Smith, James E.: The Wisdom Literature and Psalms. Joplin, Mo.: College Press Pub.Co., 1996, S. Pr 25:6-10

62. Richards, Lawrence O.: The Bible Readers Companion. electronic ed. Wheaton : VictorBooks, 1991; Published in electronic form by Logos Research Systems, 1996, S. 393

63. Carson, D. A.: New Bible Commentary: 21st Century Edition. 4th ed. Leicester, England; Downers Grove, Ill., USA : Inter-Varsity Press, 1994, S. Pr 25:8

64. Spence-Jones, H. D. M. (Hrsg.): The Pulpit Commentary: Proverbs. Bellingham, WA : Logos Research Systems, Inc., 2004, S. 480

65. Wiersbe, Warren W.: Wiersbe's Expository Outlines on the Old Testament. Wheaton, IL : Victor Books, 1993, S. Pr 25:1

66. Henry, Matthew: Matthew Henry's Commentary on the Whole Bible : Complete and Unabridged in One Volume. Peabody : Hendrickson, 1996, c1991, S. Pr 18:8

67. Reyburn, William David; Fry, Euan McG.: A Handbook on Proverbs. New York : United Bible Societies, 2000 (UBS Handbook Series; Helps for Translators), S. 545

68. Smith, James E.: The Wisdom Literature and Psalms. Joplin, Mo. : College Press Pub. Co., 1996, S. Pr 25:6-10

69. Spence-Jones, H. D. M. (Hrsg.): The Pulpit Commentary: Proverbs. Bellingham, WA : Logos Research Systems, Inc., 2004, S. 480

70. Charles Bridges, An Exposition of Proverbs, (Grand Rapids: Zondervan, 1959), pgs. 466-467.

71. Wiersbe, Warren W.: The Bible Exposition Commentary. Wheaton, Ill. : Victor Books, 1996, c1989, S. Mt 18:15

72. Carson, D. A.: New Bible Commentary : 21st Century Edition. 4th ed. Leicester, England; Downers Grove, Ill., USA : Inter-Varsity Press, 1994, S. Mt 18:15

73. Walvoord, John F. ; Zuck, Roy B. ; Dallas Theological Seminary: The Bible Knowledge Commentary : An Exposition of the Scriptures. Wheaton, IL : Victor Books, 1983-c1985, S. 2:62

74. Lenski, R. C. H., The Interpretation of St. Mathew's Gospel, (Minneapolis: Ausburg, 1964), pgs. 698-702.

75. Hendriksen, William ; Kistemaker, Simon J.: New Testament Commentary : Exposition of the Gospel According to Matthew. Grand Rapids : Baker Book House, 1953-2001 (New Testament Commentary 9), S. 698

76. Willmington, H. L.: Willmington's Bible Handbook. Wheaton, Ill. : Tyndale House Publishers, 1997, S. 538

77. Jamieson, Robert ; Fausset, A. R. ; Fausset, A. R. ; Brown, David ; Brown, David: A Commentary, Critical and Explanatory, on the Old and New Testaments. Oak Harbor, WA : Logos Research Systems, Inc., 1997, S. Mt 18:15

78. Wiersbe, Warren W.: The Bible Exposition Commentary. Wheaton, Ill. : Victor Books, 1996, c1989, S. Mt 18:15

79. Calvin, John, Harmony of Matthew, Mark, and Luke, ibid., pgs. 352-353, 355.

80. Morey, Robert A.: The Encyclopedia of Practical Christianity. PO Box 240, Millerstown, PA 17062: Christian Scholars Press, 2004, S. 454

81. Lenski, op. cit., p. 703.

82. Henry, Matthew: Matthew Henry's Commentary on the Whole Bible :

Complete and Unabridged in One Volume. Peabody : Hendrickson, 1996, c1991, S. 1 Ti 5:17

83. Walvoord, John F. ; Zuck, Roy B. ; Dallas Theological Seminary: The Bible Knowledge Commentary : An Exposition of the Scriptures. Wheaton, IL : Victor Books, 1983-c1985, S. 2:744

84. Wiersbe, Warren W.: The Bible Exposition Commentary. Wheaton, Ill. : Victor Books, 1996, c1989, S. 1 Ti 5:17

85. Lange, John Peter ; Schaff, Philip ; van Oosterzee, J. J. ; Washburn, E. A. ; Harwood, E.: A Commentary on the Holy Scriptures : 1 & 2 Timothy. Bellingham, WA : Logos Research Systems, Inc., 2008, S. 64

86. Jamieson, Robert ; Fausset, A. R. ; Fausset, A. R. ; Brown, David ; Brown, David: A Commentary, Critical and Explanatory, on the Old and New Testaments. Oak Harbor, WA : Logos Research Systems, Inc., 1997, S. 1 Ti 5:19

87. Carson, D. A.: New Bible Commentary : 21st Century Edition. 4th ed. Leicester, England; Downers Grove, Ill., USA : Inter-Varsity Press, 1994, S. 1 Ti 5:17

88. Richards, Lawrence O.: The Bible Readers Companion. electronic ed. Wheaton : Victor Books, 1991; Published in electronic form by Logos Research Systems, 1996, S. 837

89. Hendriksen, William ; Kistemaker, Simon J.: New Testament Commentary : Exposition of the Pastoral Epistles. Grand Rapids : Baker Book House, 1953-2001 (New Testament Commentary 4), S. 182

90. Knight, George W.: The Pastoral Epistles : A Commentary on the Greek Text. Grand Rapids, Mich.; Carlisle, England : W.B. Eerdmans; Paternoster Press, 1992, S. 235

91. Calvin, John, Commentary on 1 Timothy, (Grand Rapids: Eerdmans, n.d.), eg. 1 Tim. 5:19.

92. Lenski, R. C. H., The Interpretation of St. Paul's Epistles to the Colossians, to the Thessalonians,to Timothy and Titus and to Philemon, (Minneapolis: Augsburg, 1964), pgs. 683-684

93. Hendriksen, William ; Kistemaker, Simon J.: New Testament Commentary : Exposition of I-II Thessalonians. Grand Rapids : Baker Book House, 1953-2001 (New Testament Commentary 3), S. 140

94. Vincent, Marvin Richardson: Word Studies in the New Testament. Bellingham, WA : Logos Research Systems, Inc., 2002, S. 4:51

95. Richards, Lawrence O.: The Bible Readers Companion. electronic ed. Wheaton : Victor Books, 1991; Published in electronic form by Logos Research Systems, 1996, S. 389

96. Spence-Jones, H. D. M. (Hrsg.): The Pulpit Commentary: Proverbs. Bellingham, WA : Logos Research Systems, Inc., 2004, S. 66

97. Carson, D. A.: New Bible Commentary : 21st Century Edition. 4th ed. Leicester, England; Downers Grove, Ill., USA : Inter-Varsity Press, 1994, S. Pr 6:1

98. Henry, Matthew: Matthew Henry's Commentary on the Whole Bible : Complete and Unabridged in One Volume. Peabody : Hendrickson, 1996, c1991, S. Pr 6:12

99. Lange, John Peter ; Schaff, Philip ; Zöckler, Otto ; Aiken, Charles A.: A Commentary on the Holy Scriptures : Proverbs. Bellingham, WA : Logos Research Systems, Inc., 2008, S. 85

100. Reyburn, William David ; Fry, Euan McG.: A Handbook on Proverbs. New York : United Bible Societies, 2000 (UBS Handbook Series; Helps for Translators), S. 146

101. Walvoord, John F. ; Zuck, Roy B. ; Dallas Theological Seminary: The Bible Knowledge Commentary : An Exposition of the Scriptures. Wheaton, IL : Victor Books, 1983-c1985, S. 1:914

102. Smith, James E.: The Wisdom Literature and Psalms. Joplin, Mo. : College Press Pub. Co., 1996, S. Pr 6:16-19

103. Spence-Jones, H. D. M. (Hrsg.): The Pulpit Commentary: Proverbs. Bellingham, WA : Logos Research Systems, Inc., 2004, S. 130

104. Richards, Lawrence O.: The Bible Readers Companion. electronic ed. Wheaton : Victor Books, 1991; Published in electronic form by Logos Research Systems, 1996, S. 389

105. Walvoord, John F. ; Zuck, Roy B. ; Dallas Theological Seminary: The Bible Knowledge Commentary : An Exposition of the Scriptures. Wheaton, IL : Victor Books, 1983-c1985, S. 1:926

106. Henry, Matthew: Matthew Henry's Commentary on the Whole Bible : Complete and Unabridged in One Volume. Peabody : Hendrickson, 1996, c1991, S. Pr 10:1

107. Smith, James E.: The Wisdom Literature and Psalms. Joplin, Mo. : College Press Pub. Co., 1996, S. Pr 10:6-21

108. Walvoord, John F. ; Zuck, Roy B. ; Dallas Theological Seminary: The Bible Knowledge Commentary : An Exposition of the Scriptures. Wheaton, IL : Victor Books, 1983-c1985, S. 1:927

109. Henry, Matthew: Matthew Henry's Commentary on the Whole Bible : Complete and Unabridged in One Volume. Peabody : Hendrickson, 1996, c1991, S. Pr 10:18

110. Lange, John Peter ; Schaff, Philip ; Zöckler, Otto ; Aiken, Charles A.: A Commentary on the Holy Scriptures : Proverbs. Bellingham, WA : Logos Research Systems, Inc., 2008, S. 114

111. Reyburn, William David ; Fry, Euan McG.: A Handbook on Proverbs. New York : United Bible Societies, 2000 (UBS Handbook Series; Helps for Translators), S. 628

112. Henry, Matthew: Matthew Henry's Commentary on the Whole Bible : Complete and Unabridged in One Volume. Peabody : Hendrickson, 1996, c1991, S. Pr 11:9

113. Smith, James E.: The Wisdom Literature and Psalms. Joplin, Mo. : College Press Pub. Co., 1996, S. Pr 11:1-11

114. Walvoord, John F. ; Zuck, Roy B. ; Dallas Theological Seminary: The Bible Knowledge Commentary : An Exposition of the Scriptures. Wheaton, IL : Victor Books, 1983-c1985, S. 1:914

115. Henry, Matthew: Matthew Henry's Commentary on the Whole Bible : Complete and Unabridged in One Volume. Peabody : Hendrickson, 1996, c1991, S. Pr 11:12

116. Lange, John Peter ; Schaff, Philip ; Zöckler, Otto ; Aiken, Charles A.: A Commentary on the Holy Scriptures : Proverbs. Bellingham, WA : Logos Research Systems, Inc., 2008, S.121

117. Keil, Carl Friedrich ; Delitzsch, Franz: Commentary on the Old Testament. Peabody, MA :Hendrickson, 2002, S. 6:171-172

118. Carson, D. A.: New Bible Commentary : 21st Century Edition. 4th ed. Leicester, England; Downers Grove, Ill., USA : Inter-Varsity Press, 1994, S. Pr 12:5

119. Henry, Matthew: Matthew Henry's Commentary on the Whole Bible : Complete and Unabridged in One Volume. Peabody : Hendrickson, 1996, c1991, S. Pr 12:6

120. Spence-Jones, H. D. M. (Hrsg.): The Pulpit Commentary: Proverbs. Bellingham, WA: Logos Research Systems, Inc., 2004, S. 234

121. Wiersbe, Warren W.: Wiersbe's Expository Outlines on the Old Testament. Wheaton, IL :Victor Books, 1993, S. Pr 12:1

122. Smith, James E.: The Wisdom Literature and Psalms. Joplin, Mo. : College Press Pub. Co., 1996, S. Pr 12:16-26

123. Henry, Matthew: Matthew Henry's Commentary on the Whole Bible : Complete and Unabridged in One Volume. Peabody : Hendrickson, 1996, c1991, S. Pr 12:18

124. Walvoord, John F. ; Zuck, Roy B. ; Dallas Theological Seminary: The Bible Knowledge Commentary : An Exposition

of the Scriptures. Wheaton, IL : Victor Books, 1983-c1985, S. 1:934-935

125. Jamieson, Robert ; Fausset, A. R. ; Fausset, A. R. ; Brown, David ; Brown, David: A Commentary, Critical and Explanatory, on the Old and New Testaments. Oak Harbor, WA : Logos Research Systems, Inc., 1997, S. Pr 14:5

126. Henry, Matthew: Matthew Henry's Commentary on the Whole Bible : Complete and Unabridged in One Volume. Peabody : Hendrickson, 1996, c1991, S. Pr 14:6

127. Walvoord, John F. ; Zuck, Roy B. ; Dallas Theological Seminary: The Bible Knowledge Commentary : An Exposition of the Scriptures. Wheaton, IL : Victor Books, 1983-c1985, S. 1:935

128. Henry, Matthew: Matthew Henry's Commentary on the Whole Bible : Complete and Unabridged in One Volume. Peabody : Hendrickson, 1996, c1991, S. Pr 14:15129. Reyburn, William David ; Fry, Euan McG.: A Handbook on Proverbs. New York : United Bible Societies, 2000 (UBS Handbook Series; Helps for Translators), S. 314

130. Spence-Jones, H. D. M. (Hrsg.): The Pulpit Commentary: Proverbs. Bellingham, WA : Logos Research Systems, Inc., 2004, S. 272

131. Walvoord, John F. ; Zuck, Roy B. ; Dallas Theological Seminary: The Bible

215

Knowledge Commentary : An Exposition of the Scriptures. Wheaton, IL : Victor Books, 1983-c1985, S. 1:937

132. Reyburn, William David ; Fry, Euan McG.: A Handbook on Proverbs. New York : United Bible Societies, S 329

133. Henry, Matthew: Matthew Henry's Commentary on the Whole Bible : Complete and Unabridged in One Volume. Peabody : Hendrickson, 1996, c1991, S. Pr 15:4UBS Handbook Series; Helps for Translators), S. 326

134. Reyburn, William David ; Fry, Euan McG.: A Handbook on Proverbs. New York : United Bible Societies, S 329

135. Henry, Matthew: Matthew Henry's Commentary on the Whole Bible : Complete and Unabridged in One Volume. Peabody : Hendrickson, 1996, c1991, S. Pr 16:27

136. Walvoord, John F. ; Zuck, Roy B. ; Dallas Theological Seminary: The Bible Knowledge Commentary : An Exposition of the Scriptures. Wheaton, IL : Victor Books, 1983-c1985, S. 1:941

137. Smith, James E.: The Wisdom Literature and Psalms. Joplin, Mo.: College Press Pub. Co., 1996, S. Pr 16:26-30

138. Spence-Jones, H. D. M. (Hrsg.): The Pulpit Commentary: Proverbs. Bellingham, WA : Logos Research Systems, Inc., 2004, S. 315

139. Henry, Matthew: Matthew Henry's Commentary on the Whole Bible : Complete and Unabridged in One Volume. Peabody : Hendrickson, 1996, c1991, S. Pr 17:4

140. Reyburn, William David ; Fry, Euan McG.: A Handbook on Proverbs. New York : United Bible Societies, 2000 (UBS Handbook Series; Helps for Translators), S. 367

141. Walvoord, John F. ; Zuck, Roy B. ; Dallas Theological Seminary: The Bible Knowledge Commentary : An Exposition of the Scriptures. Wheaton, IL : Victor Books, 1983-c1985, S. 1:942

142. Smith, James E.: The Wisdom Literature and Psalms. Joplin, Mo.: College Press Pub. Co., 1996, S. Pr 17:1-9

143. Garrett, Duane A.: Proverbs, Ecclesiastes, Song of Songs. electronic ed. Nashville : Broadman & Holman Publishers, 2001, c1993 (Logos Library System; The New American Commentary 14), S. 158

144. Henry, Matthew: Matthew Henry's Commentary on the Whole Bible : Complete and Unabridged in One Volume. Peabody : Hendrickson, 1996, c1991, S. Pr 17:9

145. Garrett, Duane A.: Proverbs, Ecclesiastes, Song of Songs. electronic ed. Nashville : Broadman & Holman Publishers, 2001, c1993 (Logos Library

System; The New American Commentary 14), S. 161

146. Reyburn, William David ; Fry, Euan McG.: A Handbook on Proverbs. New York : United Bible Societies, 2000 (UBS Handbook Series; Helps for Translators), S. 370

147. Walvoord, John F. ; Zuck, Roy B. ; Dallas Theological Seminary: The Bible Knowledge Commentary : An Exposition of the Scriptures. Wheaton, IL : Victor Books, 1983-c1985, S. 1:942

148. Spence-Jones, H. D. M. (Hrsg.): The Pulpit Commentary: Proverbs. Bellingham, WA : Logos Research Systems, Inc., 2004, S. 332

149. Smith, James E.: The Wisdom Literature and Psalms. Joplin, Mo.: College Press Pub. Co., 1996, S. Pr 18:1-8

150. Walvoord, John F. ; Zuck, Roy B. ; Dallas Theological Seminary: The Bible Knowledge Commentary : An Exposition of the Scriptures. Wheaton, IL : Victor Books, 1983-c1985, S. 1:944

151. Henry, Matthew: Matthew Henry's Commentary on the Whole Bible : Complete and Unabridged in One Volume. Peabody : Hendrickson, 1996, c1991, S. Pr 18:8

152. Henry, Matthew: Matthew Henry's Commentary on the Whole Bible : Complete and Unabridged in One

Volume. Peabody : Hendrickson, 1996, c1991, S. Pr 18:13

153. Henry, Matthew: Matthew Henry's Commentary on the Whole Bible : Complete and Unabridged in One Volume. Peabody : Hendrickson, 1996, c1991, S. Pr 18:17

154. Smith, James E.: The Wisdom Literature and Psalms. Joplin, Mo.: College Press Pub. Co., 1996, S. Pr 18:15-24

155. Henry, Matthew: Matthew Henry's Commentary on the Whole Bible : Complete and Unabridged in One Volume. Peabody : Hendrickson, 1996, c1991, S. Pr 20:19

156. Smith, James E.: The Wisdom Literature and Psalms. Joplin, Mo.: College Press Pub. Co., 1996, S. Pr 20:13-19

157. Walvoord, John F. ; Zuck, Roy B. ; Dallas Theological Seminary: The Bible Knowledge Commentary : An Exposition of the Scriptures. Wheaton, IL : Victor Books, 1983-c1985, S. 1:959

158. Richards, Lawrence O.: The Bible Readers Companion. electronic ed. Wheaton : Victor Books, 1991; Published in electronic form by Logos Research Systems, 1996, S. 393

159. Henry, Matthew: Matthew Henry's Commentary on the Whole Bible : Complete and Unabridged in One

Volume. Peabody : Hendrickson, 1996, c1991, S. Pr 24:28

160. Carson, D. A.: New Bible Commentary: 21st Century Edition. 4th ed. Leicester, England; Downers Grove, Ill., USA : Inter-Varsity Press, 1994, S. Pr 25:8

161. Spence-Jones, H. D. M. (Hrsg.): The Pulpit Commentary: Proverbs. Bellingham, WA : Logos Research Systems, Inc., 2004, S. 480

162. Henry, Matthew: Matthew Henry's Commentary on the Whole Bible: Complete and Unabridged in One Volume. Peabody: Hendrickson, 1996, c1991, S. Pr 25:8.

163. Wiersbe, Warren W.: Wiersbe's Expository Outlines on the Old Testament. Wheaton, IL :Victor Books, 1993, S. Pr 25:1

164. Reyburn, William David; Fry, Euan McG.: A Handbook on Proverbs. New York : United Bible Societies, 2000 (UBS Handbook Series; Helps for Translators), S. 545

165. Smith, James E.: The Wisdom Literature and Psalms. Joplin, Mo.: College Press Pub. Co., 1996, S. Pr 25:6-10

166. Spence-Jones, H. D. M. (Hrsg.): The Pulpit Commentary: Proverbs. Bellingham, WA : Logos Research Systems, Inc., 2004, S. 480

167. Henry, Matthew: Matthew Henry's Commentary on the Whole Bible : Complete and Unabridged in One Volume. Peabody : Hendrickson, 1996, c1991, S. Pr 26:17

168. Charles Bridges, An Exposition of Proverbs, (Grand Rapids: Zondervan, 1959), pgs. 466-467.

169. Walvoord, John F. ; Zuck, Roy B. ; Dallas Theological Seminary: The Bible Knowledge Commentary : An Exposition of the Scriptures. Wheaton, IL : Victor Books, 1983-c1985, S. 1:962

170. Garrett, Duane A.: Proverbs, Ecclesiastes, Song of Songs. electronic ed. Nashville : Broadman & Holman Publishers, 2001, c1993 (Logos Library System; The New American Commentary 14), S. 214

171. Smith, James E.: The Wisdom Literature and Psalms. Joplin, Mo.: College Press Pub. Co., 1996, S. Pr 26:22-26

172. Walvoord, John F. ; Zuck, Roy B. ; Dallas Theological Seminary: The Bible Knowledge Commentary : An Exposition of the Scriptures. Wheaton, IL : Victor Books, 1983-c1985, S. 1:963

173. Henry, Matthew: Matthew Henry's Commentary on the Whole Bible : Complete and Unabridged in One Volume. Peabody : Hendrickson, 1996, c1991, S. Pr 29:9

174. Reyburn, William David ; Fry, Euan McG.: A Handbook on Proverbs. New York : United Bible Societies, 2000 (UBS Handbook Series; Helps for Translators), S. 608

175. Smith, James E.: The Wisdom Literature and Psalms. Joplin, Mo.: College Press Pub. Co., 1996, S. Pr 29:8-9

176. Spence-Jones, H. D. M. (Hrsg.): The Pulpit Commentary: Proverbs. Bellingham, WA : Logos Research Systems, Inc., 2004, S. 554

177. Garrett, Duane A.: Proverbs, Ecclesiastes, Song of Songs. electronic ed. Nashville : Broadman & Holman Publishers, 2001, c1993 (Logos Library System; The New American Commentary 14), S. 238

178. Walvoord, John F. ; Zuck, Roy B. ; Dallas Theological Seminary: The Bible Knowledge Commentary : An Exposition of the Scriptures. Wheaton, IL : Victor Books, 1983-c1985, S. 1:970

179. Carson, D. A.: New Bible Commentary : 21st Century Edition. 4th ed. Leicester, England; Downers Grove, Ill., USA : Inter-Varsity Press, 1994, S. Pr 30:10

180. Reyburn, William David ; Fry, Euan McG.: A Handbook on Proverbs. New York : United Bible Societies, 2000 (UBS Handbook Series; Helps for Translators), S. 628

181. Walvoord, John F. ; Zuck, Roy B. ; Dallas Theological Seminary: The Bible Knowledge Commentary : An Exposition of the Scriptures. Wheaton, IL : Victor Books, 1983-c1985, S. 1:953

182. Henry, Matthew: Matthew Henry's Commentary on the Whole Bible : Complete and Unabridged in One Volume. Peabody : Hendrickson, 1996, c1991, S. Pr 22:10

183. Reyburn, William David ; Fry, Euan McG.: A Handbook on Proverbs. New York : United Bible Societies, 2000 (UBS Handbook Series; Helps for Translators), S. 467

184. Garrett, Duane A.: Proverbs, Ecclesiastes, Song of Songs. electronic ed. Nashville : Broadman & Holman Publishers, 2001, c1993 (Logos Library System; The New American Commentary 14), S. 189

185. Spence-Jones, H. D. M. (Hrsg.): The Pulpit Commentary: Proverbs. Bellingham, WA : Logos Research Systems, Inc., 2004, S. 423

186. Jay E. Adams, The Christian Counselor's Manual, (P & R: 1973), pgs. 57-59.

Breinigsville, PA USA
03 December 2009
228450BV00006B/5/P